The Year of the Poet XI

May 2024

The Poetry Posse

inner child press, ltd.

The Poetry Posse 2024

Gail Weston Shazor
Shareef Abdur Rasheed
Teresa E. Gallion
hülya n. yılmaz
Noreen Snyder
Tzemin Ition Tsai
Elizabeth Esguerra Castillo
Jackie Davis Allen
Mutawaf Shaheed
Caroline 'Ceri' Nazareno
Ashok K. Bhargava
Alicja Maria Kuberska
Swapna Behera
Albert 'Infinite' Carrasco
Michelle Joan Barulich
Eliza Segiet
William S. Peters, Sr.

~ * ~

In order to maintain each poet's authentic voice, this volume has not undergone the scrutiny of editing. Please take time to indulge each contributor for their own creativity and aspirations to convey their uniqueness.

hülya n. yılmaz, Ph.D.
Director of Editing ~
Inner Child Press International

General Information

The Year of the Poet XI
May 2024 Edition

The Poetry Posse

1st Edition : 2024

Publisher Information

1st Edition : Inner Child Press
intouch@innerchildpress.com
www.innerchildpress.com

ISBN-13 : 978-1-961498-25-9 (inner child press, ltd.)

$ 12.99

WHAT WOULD LIFE BE WITHOUT A LITTLE POETRY?

Dedication

This Book is dedicated to

Humanity, Peace & Poetry

the Power of the Pen

can effectuate change!

&

The Poetry Posse

past, present & future,

our Patrons and Readers &

the Spirit of our Everlasting Muse

In the darkness of my life
I heard the music
I danced . . .
and the Light appeared
and I dance

Janet P. Caldwell

Table of Contents

The Poetry Posse

Table of Contents . . . *continued*

Foreword

Renowned Poets

Makhanlal Chaturvedi

"I don't wish to be adorned as an ornament of a beautiful bride
I have no craving to be a gift presented to the beloved,
I don't cherish to be placed on the casket or grave of great kings,
I never desire to be on the heads of the idols of Gods,
dear gardener rather pluck me and be throw me on the road
where the soldiers march forward to sacrifice their heads
for their motherland!"

"A flower's wishes" by Makhanlal Chatturvedi

The above stanza is the translated version of the famous Hindi poem PUSHPA KI ABHILASHA written by Padma Bhusan Pandit Makhan Lal Chaturvedi. In this poem he expresses his feelings for his nation through a flower. The personified flower says that it is not preferable to become a garland of a beloved or to adorn the hair of beautiful women or be offered to God or on the funeral of great kings. The only wish the flower is to lie on the path on which brave soldiers pass to sacrifice their lives for the nation. 'A Flower's Wishes' is written in the Bilaspur prison, situated in present-day Chhattisgarh, was an allegorical poetry representing the nation's spirit of freedom and selfless sacrifice.

Pandit Makhan Lal Chaturvedi, was an Indian poet, writer, essayist, playwright and a journalist who is particularly remembered for his participation in India's national struggle for independence and his contribution to Chhayavaad and the Neo-romanticism movement of Hindi literature. He has taken an active part in the Non-Cooperation Movement and was jailed in 1921. His literature showed his intense desire for India's freedom from British rule.

His famous poems are "I am afraid of myself", The prisoner and the Nightingale", 'Climbing the mountain slowly" "Air," "Boon or curse", "youth", 'Immortal Nation" "Let me cry"

what do you sing?
Why do you keep going?
the cuckoo speak up!
What do you bring?
Whose message is it?

- the soldier and the cuckoo -

Pandit Makhanlal Chaturvedi (4 April 1889 – 30 January 1968), was an Indian poet and editor famous for his works such as Venu Lo Gunje Dhara, Him Kirtini Him Tarangini, Yug Charan, Sahitya Devata, etc. He was born in in a Babai [Makhan Nagar] village of Narmadapuram district of Madhya Pradesh in India on 4 April 1889. He is a writer, essayist, playwright and a journalist who is particularly remembered for his participation in

India's national struggle for Independence and his contribution to the Neo Romanticism movement of Hindi literature, known as Chhayavaad. Indian language went through a nationwide phase of romantic writing in the period between the two World Wars (1920 -1935). This phase overlapped with the nationalist movement Chhayavaad,

He became a school teacher at the age of sixteen. Later he was the editor of the nationalist journals Prabha, Pratap and Karmaveer, and was repeatedly incarcerated during the British Raj. His noted works in Hindi are *Him Kirtini*, *Him Tarangini*, *Yug Charan*, and *Sahitya Devata*, and his most noted poems are *Venu Lo Gunje Dhara*, *Deep Se Deep Jale*, *Kaisa Chhand Banaa Deti hai*, *Agnipath* and *Pushp ki Abhilaashaa*

In his memory Madhya Pradesh Cultural Council organizes the annual 'Makhanlal Chaturvedi Samaroh', since 1987, besides awarding the annual 'Makhanlal Chaturvedi Puraskar' for excellence in poetry by an Indian poet. The Makhanlal Chaturvedi Rashtriya Patrakarita Vishwavidyalaya is at Bhopal in Madhya Pradesh which has been named in his honour. His poems displayed his unconditional love and respect towards his country and that is why he was also referred to as a true Indian spirit. Later, he was the editor of the nationalist journals *Prabha*, Pratap and *Karmaveer*, and was repeatedly incarcerated during the British Rule. After the Indian independence, he refrained from seeking a position in the government, instead continuing to speak and write against social evils and in support of an exploitation-free, equitable society as envisioned by Mahatma Gandhi

Chayavad is a particular emotional approach with philosophical experience having a particular style in an era of poetry where the supernatural is portrayed through cosmic love and cosmic experiences are depicted through supernatural love. In such poetry, nature is presented in human form. Pundit Makhanlal Chaturvedi used a new style in his writing. This style is called the Neo-romanticism style of the Chhayavaad era. He is the first winner of Sahitya Akademi Award and the recipient of Pdama Bhusan the third highest civilian award in the Republic India

They keep climbing moment after moment,
without a sound, crying!
Days, months and seasons come quietly and
without invitation
on their own;
People say that I have advanced in age,
but I am always descending, my friend!
I am afraid of myself, my friend!

(the English translated version of his Hindi poem I am afraid of myself, my friend)

Brother, don't tease me,
let me cry freely. Let
this heart of stone
be washed with tears

(Let me cry)

The Inner Child Press with its mission of *building bridges of cultural understanding* takes the responsibility for global peace and harmony through poetry with International Anthologies.

We respect the land, nature, folk tales, culture, music, literature, perceptions, ideas, thoughts, language, art, artisans and all ethnic groups of the world beyond the borders.

The year 2024 was assigned and dedicated to renowned poets of the globe. Since the theme of the World Poetry Day 2024 is "standing on the shoulders of giant' we express our respect and gratitude to these iconic poets. The month of May is dedicated to Padma Bhusan pandit Makhanlal Chatturvedi ji.

Literature has undergone a tectonic change. We express our deep reverence to all for they are the apostles of a time zone who have solved the situations, saved human lives and helped the economic, cultural social growth of society.

Poetry is the living song of human race ....
When the whole world is silent even one voice becomes powerful. We respect the humanity. We respect the voice that speaks for justice. We admire the voice that speaks for growth of civilisation. We respect coexistence beyond any disparities. We appreciate the designers of literature and language.

Our deep reverence to Pandit Makhanlal Chaturvedi; one of the pioneers of Chhayavad and Neo Romanticism.

Long live global peace ….

Swapna Behera

Cultural Ambassador of India and South East Asia for Inner Child Press International.

Now Available

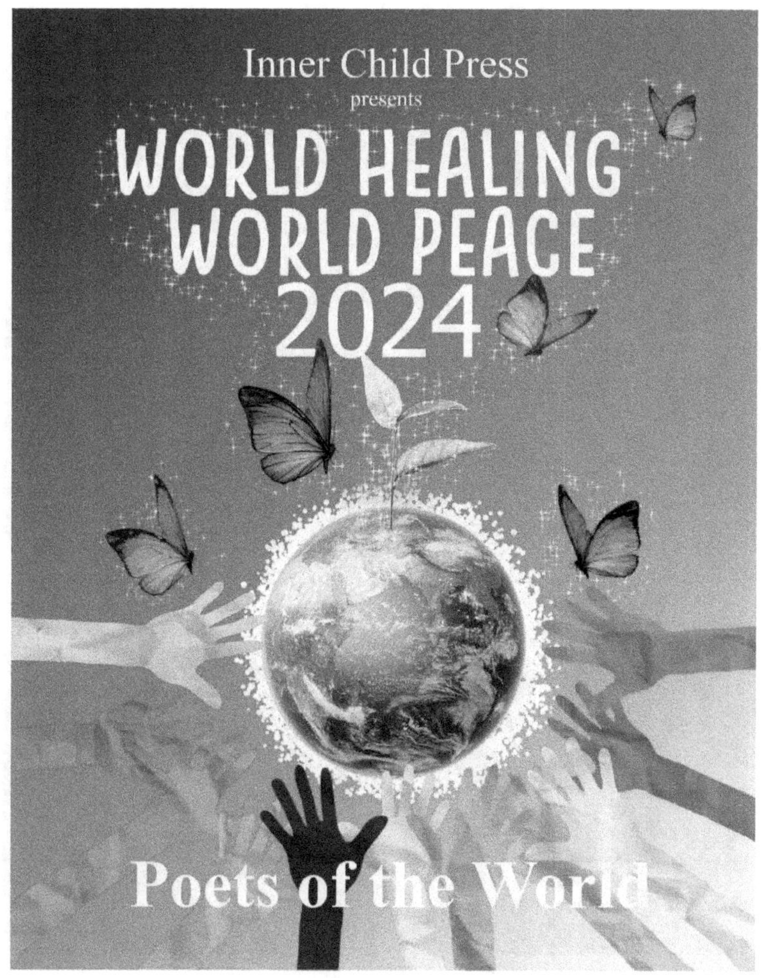
Inner Child Press
presents
WORLD HEALING
WORLD PEACE
2024
Poets of the World

www.innerchildpress.com/world-healing-world-peace-poetry

Now Available

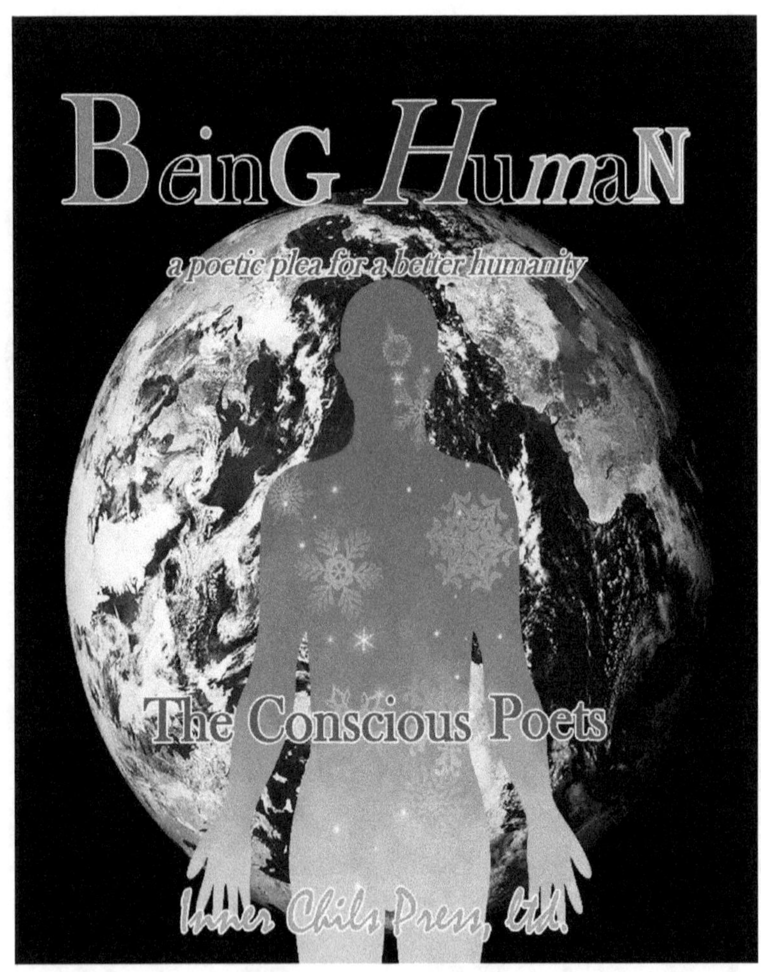
BeinG HumaN
a poetic plea for a better humanity
The Conscious Poets
Inner Child Press, ltd.

www.innerchildpress.com/now-open-4-submission

Preface

We, **Inner Child Press International, The Year of the Poet** and **The Poetry Posse** welcome you.

WOW . . . a decade +. We continue to be excited as we have now crossed over into our 11th year of **The Year of the Poet**.

This particular year we have chosen to feature renowned poets of history. We do hope you enjoy. Read ~ Learn.

For those of you who are not familiar with our story, back in 2013, a few of us poets got together with the simple intention of producing a book a month. That was our challenge. Since that time the enterprise has blossomed and brought forth a fruit that seems to keep on growing as evidenced as we enter 2023.

Our purpose is simple. Through our lyrical words and verse, we not only wish to share our poetic works, but we also have the poetic naiveté to believe that we can assist in the growth of consciousness of the things that have an effect our collective humanity. Therefore, we welcome your readership. For more about what we are attempting to accomplish, have a look at our Publishing Web Site . . . www.innerchildpress.com. If you would like to know a bit more about this particular endeavor please stop by for a visit at :

www.innerchildpress.com/the-year-of-the-poet

Over the years, Inner Child Press has been socially active to bring awareness and catalog through literature the things that have an impact upon our world and its inhabitants. We have solicited, produced, underwritten and published quite a few volumes to that end. For more insight you may wish to visit : www.innerchildpress.com/the-anthology-market. If you are a writer, poet, or activist, you would be advised to keep a eye out for upcoming volumes should you desire to participate. All readers are welcomed as well. Note, that there is a myriad of published volumes that are available as a FREE PDF download as well as available for purchase at affordable prices.

We at this time extend to you our well wishes for your own personal journey and hope that you consider including us as a travel companion.

Bless Up

Bill

William S. Peters, Sr.

Publisher
Inner Child Press International
www.innerchildpress.com

Renowned Poets

Pandit Makhanlal Chaturvedi

also known as

Makhan Lal Chaturvedi

and

Pandit ji

1889 ~ 1968

May 2024

The Flower's Wish

I don't desire to adorn a fair maiden's ornaments,
I don't desire to be an attractive gift to a beloved,
I don't desire to be on the death bed of great kings,
I don't desire to be on idols of Gods,
I'd rather be plucked to be thrown on the path,
On which march the braves to give their life for their motherland!

* *English translation by Savita Gupta*

Original Poem Title: "Pushp ki Abhilasha"

Makhanlal Chaturvedi composed "Pushp ki Abhilasha" before India's independence from the British on August 15, 1947. Pandit ji himself was directly involved in the struggles for freedom. He had participated actively in the Non-Cooperation Movement and was jailed in 1921. In its entirety, his literary work showed his intense yearning for India's freedom from British rule.

The significance of the poet for Indian literature has been marked, among numerous other recognitions, by India's first university for journalism and mass communication; namely, the public university Makhanlal Chaturvedi National University of Journalism and Communication in Bhopal, Madhya Pradesh, India—established in 1992 and named after Makhan Lal Chaturvedi.

Chhayavaad, the Neo-romanticism movement of Hindi literature, owes its advancement to Makhanlal Chaturvedi. A staunch patriot, poet, writer, and journalist, Pandit ji was and still is celebrated in India on account of his unwavering encouragement and persuasion of the masses to protest against the disruptive and tyrannical nature of the British regime. Without branching out into politics at any point in his life, Chaturvedi is known to have molded his identity as a writer. His nationalistic poems that favor Mahatma Gandhi's vision, thus speak of an equitable society free from exploitation, were based on a novel writing style, signifying the Chhayavaad era's neo-romanticism style. Pandit ji's most prominent poems include , "Pushp ki Abhilasha", "Venu Lo Gunje Dhara", "Deep se Deep Jale", "Agnipath", "Amar Rashtra Kavita", and "Him Tarangini". In 1955, he was awarded the first Sahitya Akademi Award in Hindi for "Him Tarangini".

A brief side note seems to be called for at this juncture; or better yet, regarding the second word of the most frequently cited poem by Chaturvedi. It appears that it presents quite a challenge when our West-focused minds are concerned (i.e., the wrongful reference to "pervert" in Telugu). A look into the etymological origin of "Tarangini", however, results in a succinctly defined natural element: "river", with its meaning being identical in Sanskrit, Hindi, Telugu, etc. "Tarang", equating the English word "a wave or ripple", and "Tarangini" explicating "the water body that has waves or ripples". Unlike the terribly misleading translation from Telugu as mentioned above, "Tarangini" often portrays "a woman who is like a wave" or "one who is wave-like." In fact, the name, as several sources emphasize, draws a poetic comparison to the graceful and fluid movements of waves in the ocean. The indisputable richness of the language of focus here may also be seen in yet another meaning of the same second word in Pandit ji's famed poem: "Tarangini" referring to an opera that is highly suitable for dance drama which has been performed over the last two centuries by Indian classical dancers.

Let us hope jointly for not even a single word of our poems ever being subjected to missed translations.

hülya n. yılmaz, Ph.D.

Professor Emerita, Liberal Arts (Penn State, U.S.A.)
Director of Editing Services, Inner Child Press International (U.S.A.)

Selected Sources:

Encyclopedia Britannica. South Asian Arts. The Classical Period
kavishala.com. Makhanlal Chaturvedi. Poems, Stories
guruguha.org. Tarangini. The Story of a Quaint Beauty
Cutting Chai. Savita Gupta
Wikipedia. Makhanlal Chaturvedi National University of Journalism and Communication

Poets . . .
sowing seeds in the
Conscious Garden of Life,
that those who have yet to come
may enjoy the Flowers.

Poets, Writers . . . know that we are the enchanting magicians that nourishes the seeds of dreams and thoughts . . . it is our words that entice the hearts and minds of others to believe there is something grand about the possibilities that life has to offer and our words tease it forth into action . . . for you are the Poet, the Writer to whom the Gift of Words has been entrusted . . .

~ wsp

poetry is . . .
India INK

Poetry succeeds where instruction fails.

~ wsp

Advisory Board

World Healing, World Peace Foundation

human beings for humanity

2024

worldhealingworldpeacefoundation.org

Gail
Weston
Shazor

Gail Weston Shazor is a lover of words. She is fond of the arcane, unusual and the not yet words.

Coining words at an early age, there was often a bit of trouble with teachers, but she always had her mother and aunt to back up her choices in expression. Born in Mississippi, she spent her early years with her grandparents. Each of the four left very careful influences on her pre-schooling. She learned in turn how women worked in and out of the home and how men worked in and out of the home to support the family. She learned that a lack of proper schooling was not the only way to learn and understanding life was a great teacher. As in most rural families of color, women had a greater chance of formal learning. Both of Gail's grandmothers read out loud to the family whether it was the bible or the newspapers and important documents to their spouses.

Gail Weston Shazor has authored (so far) Notes from the Blue Roof, A Overstanding of an Imperfect Love, HeartSongs and Lies My Grandfather's Told Me. The number of anthologies is too many to list with the premier accomplishment of one of the contributors to The Year of The Poet. Gail will always lend her ink to community projects and will purchase the books of fellow poets in the Inner Child Press family.

Ready or Not

The bombs fall over bricks
Exploding the grass and mud
Of that which we built
To separate one from another
No furrowed earth
No wasted harvest
And yet we blame
The unquality of life
On him/her/they
Dem ovah der
It's here
It's us
Hot or cold war
Our religion
Our hearts
Has been colonialized
To a high water mark
The only thing left is
Decolonialization
The breaking up
Of the build up
We do not have enough fingers
To dam the holes
The flood is coming
Ready or Not

PallBearer

You drift slowly
In this moment
Trailing fingers
In the current
Ignoring the spray
Of the many voices
Buffeting the air
Solemnity rides along
The creases in your jacket
And darkness is carried
From knee to knee
Of the trousers
Worn too often in this season
Of faithful service
To those beside you
You have been carefully
Tended to this day
With a quietness
And gentle touches
To ease the passage
For the weight you carry
Is borne in your heart
Not to be measured
In the solidity of stones
For at the waning of life
You bear peace.

Thoughts out Loud

Today I am wondering
Thinking and pondering
If I let go and listen
Will you hear me?
Hear my heartbeat?
I cannot enjoy not being in love
Between the differences
Of understanding
Who I am with you
And who I am
In the shadows of alone
I never meant to fall
Backwards
Gasping for air
And experiencing bliss
Not able to wrap my head
Around your heart
Can you hear it?
I am praying soundlessly
Pleading for just
A little more
And lying to God, though He knows it
I can't get enough
Of feeling like this
Or feeling like that
Sensing your touch across my memory
Some things I understand
I must experience you
Drunken on my tongue
Speaking in whispers
Living loud enough
For the neighbors to hear

And shake their heads
Not understanding
That love is
Ringing
Out loud
Do you see me?

Alicja
Maria
Kuberska

Alicja Maria Kuberska – awarded Polish poetess, novelist, journalist, editor.

She is a member of the Polish Writers Associations in Warsaw, Poland and IWA Bogdani, Albania. She is also a member of directors' board of Soflay Literature Foundation, Our Poetry Archive (India) and Cultural Ambassador for Poland (Inner Child Press, USA)

Her poems have been published in numerous anthologies and magazines in : Poland, Czech Republic, Slovakia, Hungary,Ukraina, Belgium, Bulgaria, Albania, Spain, the UK, Italy, the USA, Canada, the UK, Argentina, Chile, Peru, Israel, Turkey, India, Uzbekistan, South Korea, Taiwan, China, Australia, South Africa, Zambia, Nigeria

She received two medals - the Nosside UNESCO Competition in Italy (2015) and European Academy of Science Arts and Letters in France (2017). Ahe also received a reward of international literary competition in Italy „ Tra le parole e 'elfinito" (2018). She was announced a poet of the 2017 year by Soflay Literature Foundation (2018).She also received : Bolesław Prus Prize Poland (2019), Culture Animator Poland (2019) and first prize Premio Internazionale di Poesia Poseidonia- Paestrum Italy (2019).

Pandit Makhanlal Chaturvedi

The poet carries a gun and shoots words
- pierces the armour in people's hearts,
breaks indifference into pieces,
dispels doubts and queries.

It's a strange weapon
- invisible but effective,
dangerous to enemies.

The fight for the homeland's independence
creates multicoloured words
and like a chameleon
it changes colours in the stanzas
black – angry
red – fiery
green – full of hope

What can a poet do?
Nothing and everything.

The words

The words never die.
They live forever,
and remain like stones.
The said words are
as fleeting blow-balls
of thoughts.
The written words are
standing the test of time.

There is no Platon or Petrarka.
The body of Dante changed
into dust, but their words
are still alive.

The twilight

I like this moment very much,
when the sun greets the moon.
It is the end of a hard-working day
And the beginning of the night.

The twilight covers the sky
Delicately with a black veil and
slowly scatters the silver stars.
The coolness and grey of night
put out the colorful bird's singing
and wake up the noiseless bats.
The frogs and crickets
begin their evening concert.

I admire this time of transformation
As the light turns into darkness
And the day turns into night.

Jackie
Davis
Allen

Jackie Davis Allen

Jackie Davis Allen, otherwise known as Jacqueline D. Allen or Jackie Allen, grew up in the Cumberland Mountains of Appalachia. As the next eldest daughter of a coal miner father and a stay at home mother, she was the first in her family to attend and graduate from college. Her siblings, in their own right, are accomplished, though she is the only one, to date, that has discovered the gift of writing.

Graduating from Radford University, with a Bachelor's of Science degree in Early Education, she taught in both public and private schools. For over a decade she taught private art classes to children both in her home and at a local Art and Framing Shop where she also sold her original soft sculptured Victorian dolls and original christening gowns.

She resides in northern Virginia with her husband, taking much needed get-aways to their mountain home near the Blue Ridge Mountains, a place that evokes memories of days spent growing up in the Appalachian Mountains.

A lover of hats, she has worn many. Following marriage to her college sweetheart, and as wife, mother, grandmother, teacher, tutor, artist, writer, poet and crafter, she is a lover of art and antiques, surrounding herself, always, with books, seeking to learn more.

In 2015 she authored *Looking for Rainbows, Poetry, Prose and Art*, and in 2017, *Dark Side of the Moon*. Both books of mostly narrative poetry were published by Inner Child Press and were edited by hulya n. yilmaz in 2019, *No Illusions. Through the Looking Glass*, which was nominated to be considered for a Pulitzer Prize by the publisher and editor of Inner Child Press, ltd.

http://www.innerchildpress.com/jackie-davis-allen.php
jackiedavisallen.com

A Literary Man, and More

Did ever a man,
Lover of country,
Of his countrymen
Dream of freedom, hope? For All?
Release from oppression?

Did not a man,
Seek it persistently?
Intentionally investing himself,
Lavishly, widely, sharing those dreams?
Across, and within his nation?

Did not this poet, writer, essayist,
Journalist, suffer incarceration?
For sharing this?
At the hands of those in power?
And yet, he carried on?

Did not this man,
Pandit ji, succeed
In seeing the blossoming,
The unfurling
Of his heart's long-held desire?

Long Past Eight-Bells

A photograph sits on my dresser.
O, that his lips might smother mine with kisses.
So, unlike the sailor occupying my mind,
He in distress, alarmed by battle's affliction.

Night and day, prayers find me on my knees,
Interceding for the weary,
Wary of impending agitation...

One train of thought here.
The other tracking the war.

O, if only I could,
I would bring thee a posy and sweet wine to sip.
Do you remember times of rendezvous
In the mountains, the golden honeysuckle?

A day chasing a baby rabbit? The sun, rain, sweet earthy scents?
Salt in hand, were we hoping to catch a bird?
Tall tales to share with laughter, to pass on to our heirs?

Flapping uniformly in the breeze,
Ghostly visions hang tenaciously onto memory's line.

Where have they all gone,
The times of our youth?
The sweet taste of childhood, the butterflies,
whose wings danced in the air?

The birds who were singing
You and I dangling over the mountain tops?
Clinging to thick vines, drunk
With the sweet intensity of the moment?

O, there's more stories I could tell,
Were they not lost, buried, like you. At sea. Alas!
Today I sleep the sleep of a time that stands still.

Bits and pieces pass as they happen.
Snatches and glimmers of a string-uncertain unwind in the air.

I am like a kite who knows not
Where the string began. Or where it will end.
O, what is to befall me?
My mind has wandered and has left me alone.

Alas, I have been transformed by the violence
Of the age, a casualty, idly to be picked up.
And placed on a shelf by kind strangers.

Am I just a faint representation of the girl I once was?
Yet the ocean still rumbles. Still roars.

I am adrift on the shore.
Someone, will you now, lift me up, draw me,
Tenderly, near unto your breast?
Does anyone hear me calling? Or am I but an apparition?

Chide me neither for my forgetfulness.
Nor for my sorrow.
Does anyone understand?

Indulge me, gently; then, call me by my name.
For it is one of the things I no longer recall.

Leading by Example

Oblivious, the children played and laughed,
In guise of twirling, spinning tops,
They smiled
At the dark clouds
That engulfed the rest of us.

The sun's golden orb, a gift to their bidding.
Played silly games,
Like one called Hide and Seek.
And, the cherished children
Lifted their voices in cheer.

Their feet danced, sweetly reminiscent
Of hymns, like music tinkling
As if from a bell tower,
Their lilting joy drifted
Above the tree-tops.

And we, beyond grief,
We the adults, brought to our knees, prayed
That sorrow's whispers of consolation
Might soon soothe
Grief's injurious wounds.

With courage, we wiped our eyes.
We smiled with the children,
Anointing them with the hope of tomorrow.
We, the adults turned away for the moment,
And joy came despite the mourning hour.

Tzemin Ition Tsai

Tzemin Ition Tsai

Dr. Tzemin Ition Tsai comes from the Republic of China(Taiwan). In addition to being a professor of literature at a university, he is more committed to writing poems, novels, and proses. He is also an editor of "Reading, Writing and Teaching" academic text, an International editor of "Contemporary dialogues" literary periodical in Macedonia, and Vice-Chairman of the International Jury of the SAHITTO INTERNATIONAL AWARD in Bangladesh, and a columnist for "Chinese Language Monthly" in Taiwan.

In a wide range of literary creations, he is particularly fond of interesting stories or novels, and writing articles or poems about the feelings of nature and human beings. He has won many national literary awards. His literary works have been anthologized and published in books, journals, and newspapers in more than 55 countries and have been translated into more than 24 languages.

That Foothold

Beneath the Bodhi tree I stand, vibrant and full of life,
Gazing into the quiet soul of the earth.
The laughter of children once danced in the air,
Now, the quiet echoes of solitude only appear by chance.
As the sun ascends, observing.
The azure sky, It reminds us, even on the darkest nights,
The gentle flow of rivers never ceases.
Destiny and cunning converse with their paths.
Unbound, uninterrupted, unhindered, free,
A spirit of victory, seeds germinate within the heart of the nation,
Crops meet, disseminating hope and courage,
With each day, every sigh,
We learn to fly, we are reborn,
Each stone bears the mark of resilience,
The quiet strength known to the humble.
A new kingdom, so precisely remembered,
Every moment, every tale,
On the scrolls of glory, embracing the promise of a bright tomorrow.

The Tiger

In the silence of the night, the roar of a tiger echoes,
Beyond the Orchid Pavilion a thousand miles away.
Sad and desolate, a deep growl,
Deep and emotional, a haunting melody.
Under the guise of the rock garden, the breeze blows,
The lush and tender touch of a lover's kiss.
In the depths of the night, the king of the forest,
Discloses a thousand tender emotions.

Moonlight and crystal-clear dew fill his heart,
He is walking silently through the land of no one.
In the deep forest, a man stands,
Embracing heaven and earth.
A roar opens up the mountains and the rivers,
Whispers of the loneliness of the night.
With a knife hidden in his eyebrows, his body is like a tiger.
He walks without fear of hardship and sits without question of the world.

His fighting spirit is a flicker in the night,
Stars in heaven fade in comparison.
He mourns his own fate,
But also feels proud and wild.

A Lone Goose's Cry Pierces Thousands Of Mountains

The desert sky is shaken by a single shadow.
The wings of a soaring bird cut through the clouds and the mountains overlap.
The peak spans ten thousand ridges, and my love for the sky is far more tragic than the sound of a single cry.
I fish alone under the lonely shadow of the cold river.
Not a single flying goose to be seen in the sky.
It still illuminates the continuation of the old road, reflecting the clarity of the river water.
Speechless flowers fly down from the sky with the wind.
Light cuts the lonely goose's bitter love in shadow, but shines through the snow on thousands of mountains.

The sea of clouds is roiling, the world is confused.
With a broken wing, where can I live between the mountains and the sea?
Normal streets have disappeared.
The mountains in the distance are still full of beauty, hidden in the infinite space.
The wild goose is willing to look back, but it is not able to survive the fireworks of the world.
The peak is independent and adjacent to the sea.
The mountains remain the same and the sea remains the same.
Falling to the galaxy, home is in my heart.
If the footsteps are firm and unyielding.

Shareef Abdur Rasheed

Shareef Abdur-Rasheed, AKA Zakir Flo was born and raised in Brooklyn, New York. His education includes Brooklyn College, Suffolk County Community College and Makkah, Saudi Arabia. He is a Veteran of the Viet Nam era, where in 1969 he reverted to his now reverently embraced Islamic Faith. He is very active in the Islamic community and beyond with his teachings, activism and his humanity.

Shareef's spiritual expression comes through the persona of "Zakir Flo" . Zakir is Arabic for "To remind". Never silent, Shareef Abdur-Rasheed is always dropping science, love, consciousness and signs of the time in rhyme.

Shareef is the Patriarch of the Abdur-Rasheed Family with 9 Children (6 Sons and 3 Daughters) and 41 Grandchildren (24 Boys and 17 Girls).

For more information about Shareef, visit his personal FaceBook Page at :

https://www.facebook.com/shareef.abdurrasheed1
https://zakirflo.wordpress.com

Chaturvedi

B:April 04, 1889
D:Jan. 30, 1968
India's national
treasure
this epic, generational
immensely gifted
artist of a variety
of genre's
poet, playwright,
essayist, journalist
voice of justice,
sanity, beauty,
advice that a nation
of hundreds of millions
needed to heed
unfortunately to often
instead, as is historically
repeated persecuted,
imprisoned
at hands of invaders,
occupiers
in spite of that this
activist never wavered,
bowed but stood out
stood up as a voice
through his art
became a thorn in the
body of these British
colonialist
the power of artful
expression
often through out

history has successfully
accomplished what
Seemed the impossible
Makhanlal Chaturvedi
Was one of this special
Group

in 'n ' out

in ' n ' out breathing what it's all about
that's what i'm taking bout...life
difference between death, life like day, night
life itself a loan entrusted to us all, just a trust
but most of us bust the trust,
oooh what's the fuss?
exactly the problem..,
ingratitude, self-destructive attitude
not to be taken lightly by politely mumbling
trite platitudes
we're talking loan of life, breathing undeserving
mercy bestowed but never owed, therefore we
owe plenty for being recipients allowed to be
participants in the benefits of what's heaven sent
though you and i know we haven't showed enough
appreciation yet
because human beings got lost forgetting who's the
boss
the one who said " Be " BAM You ' n Me!
just like that truly...life, breath, air, senses, sight, hearing,
smell, touch, taste, mind, memory, sensation
what part of that do you have no appreciation?
sooo participate in the celebration of life by...,
living right, giving thanks day ' n ' night,
yah datz right!

Like Dark Clouds..,

bring rain, pain can bring gain
thus mankind must refrain
from lusting for comfort as
struggle remains here to stay
until end of days we must embrace
another way that includes being
resolute to endure what pain comes
our way with faithful patience
each and every day
increases faith, strength, endurance
adherence to commandments
from lord of all worlds
pain purges impurities when absorbed
patiently
remembering what comes after difficulty
ease, twice as much as the pain is ease
manifests merciful reward for passing
a test
comes only from merciful lord who's
majesty and mercy stands far
above the rest who may profess to be the best
though creation can not even be an imitation
of thee creator's all-encompassing domination
as this short life no matter what's acquired
can not save you from the hour of his power
as you take your final breath
everything man-made will fade just as all
mankind has limited days to tarry
nothing here will you take to the eternal
destination but the deeds compiled
to be weighed on the scale, then only
divine mercy will determine if you passed
or failed.

either way pass or fail what comfort that
you sought to soothe will desert you and in
comparison what award awaits the faithful
earthly comfort pales, as your efforts failed
thus universal law made plain to all of us
No pain, No gain

Noreen Snyder

Noreen Snyder

Noreen Ann Snyder has been writing since she was a teenager. She writes a variety of different topics. Her favorite poetic forms are Sonnets, Blitz, Haiku, Tanka, and Free Verse. She always learning different poetic forms.

Noreen Ann Snyder is a poet, writer, and an author of five books, (four books are co-authored with her late husband, Garry A. Snyder.) Her poetry is in several Inner Child Press Anthologies. She is the founder ofThe Poetry Club on Facebook.

Makhanlal Chaturvedi

Well-loved Indian poet and writer
Through his poetry, he wrote
against the Britist rule and
want the people to stand up for their freedom.
He was awarded the first
Sahitya Akademi Award in Hindi
for his famous work, 'Him Tarangini.
Referred to as 'Yug Charan'
and that is an honor.
Yes, he was and still is a well-loved Indian poet
It's an honor to research him.

No Secrets

Sun is sleeping

Moon is guarding the Earth

Stars are guiding us in the darkness

whether we're awake or not

But God, our Father, never sleeps.

No secrets kept from our God.

He knows it all.

For Those Who Pushed Through

Rainbows represent our dreams.
Let it build up our self-esteem.
Yes, it can be fulfilled!
Just believe, and be self-willed.
There's a time when life
was simple and less strife,
we all helped each
other and to reach
out to all
without a brawl.
Rainbows
are for those
who
pushed through.

Elizabeth
E.
Castillo

Elizabeth Esguerra Castillo

Elizabeth Esguerra Castillo is a multi-awarded and an Internationally-Published Contemporary Author/Poet and a Professional Writer / Creative Writer / Feature Writer / Journalist / Travel Writer from the Philippines. She has 2 published books, "Seasons of Emotions" (UK) and "Inner Reflections of the Muse", (USA). Elizabeth is also a co-author to more than 60 international anthologies in the USA, Canada, UK, Romania, India. She is a Contributing Editor of Inner Child Magazine, USA and an Advisory Board Member of Reflection Magazine, an international literary magazine. She is a member of the American Authors Association (AAA) and PEN International.

Web links:

Facebook Fan Page

https://free.facebook.com/ElizabethEsguerraCastillo

Google Plus

https://plus.google.com/u/0/+ElizabethCastillo

The Wise Pandit

His words are immortal
Left verses of encouragement to mankind
Literary works so sublime
The world admires his works
His legacy as a wise wordsmith lives on
Ebbed in the hearts of literary enthusiasts.

Autumn

The bare and naked branches
Signify the beginning of a new frontier
Here I am pondering
A distant dream lingering
An echo sounds off the wilderness
Revelry awakens the soul
Yearning for autumn to dawn.

Musings

This is the time of mystical things
When the muse comes alive
During the week hours of the night
Breaking dawn
When only the sound of crickets can be heard
And an owl calling its mate
The muse begins it's journey
Verses come rushing in out if nowhere.

Mutawaf Shaheed

Mutawaf Shaheed

C. E. Shy has been writing since the seventh grade. He continued writing through high school, until he became more involved in sports. After his graduation, he worked at the White Motors Company where he wrote for the company's newspaper. He started a column called: "The Poet's Corner." That was his first published work.

www.innerchildpress.com/c-e-shy.php

Makhanlal Chaturved

Century turning at his feet. Just in time to repeat
phrases of the sages that he'd never meet. Trying
hard in trying times make the measure of the man.

Speaking the truth in the oppressors face not caring
about his fate. Spending some time in jail, made take
a harder stand. The people must have been listening.

Loving freedom was his voice even though he had a
Choice. Be assured the students learned from what said.
After all the Brits were gone he still kept his voice real
Strong.

Mixed Messages

Taking letters from alphabetical orders,
sending mixed emotions by arranging
and re-arranging them to say whatever,
whenever. Establishing images in the
minds of those can read them.

Then responding with the same letters
saying something or not. Who can be
reached with such speech is configured
in what they see, because they have no
understanding.

They read what they are told when scolded
by the phrases. Presented with gifts of gabs,
real words go unheard by the IQ-less. Unable
to read signs as letters go flying by.

Happy hours, becoming un-happy, can't cope
without the soaps. They could never relate to
an opera of any kind. The letters are giving
gloom, removing the glimmer that the liars
used to control.

However, you read it, tomorrow is either closer
or further away. When re-arranging any of these
letters, there is only so much you can say.

Cunning and unkind

Cunning and unkind, in one eye he's blind.
On a murderous rampage. since the beginning
of his time.

Gagging on greed taking more than he need.
Profanity, insanity add to his vanity.

Lies thick ,quick. Bathes in the blood of others
even his mother, brothers.

Heart covered in smut, unlucky in love. Demons
for pets.

Clothes soiled with piss, puss, plus us. To hell or
bust.

Retractable fangs, horns hidden by bangs sad
songs he sang.

Blowing wind in deep in his skin, hellish ideas
fester within.

Consciously cruel. His stool is his gruel.
He mocks time with crime. His bottom line's
erased. Snake venom in him.

Homicide justified. human beings mortified.
Police took stand and told a lie, he was thinking
God had died.

All his violence quantified, planet earth modified,
breathing gas, trivialized, around the world there
he go, where he stops--------- God he knows!

hülya
n.
yılmaz

Of Turkish descent, hülya n. yılmaz [sic] is Professor Emerita (Penn State, U.S.A.), Director of Editing Services (Inner Child Press International, U.S.A.), and a trilingual literary translator. Before her poetry and prose publications, she authored an extensive research book in German on cross-cultural literary influences.

Her works of literature include a trilingual collection of poems, memoirs in verse, prose poetry, short stories, a bilingual poetry book, and two books of poetry (one, co-authored). Her poetic offerings appeared in numerous anthologies of global endeavors.

hülya writes creatively to attain and nourish a comprehensive awareness for and development of our humanity.

hülya n. yılmaz, a traveler on the journey called "life" . . .

Writing Web Site
https://hulyanyilmaz.com/

Editing Web Site
https://hulyasfreelancing.com

Tarangini

"Tarangini", a river, in Sanskrit, Hindi, and Telugu,
Perverted by some irresponsible internet surfers
Into "pervert" in Telugu.

The warning label is there,
Speaking out loud:
Take translations with a grain of salt,
Such as "Tarangini",
Meaning "a wave or a ripple";
In actuality, often referring to
"a wave-like woman".

A body of water, waiting to be uncovered
Under the name "Tarangini" . . .

Labels

Who determines what is neoclassicism?

Within which periods of time does it belong?

What stylistic aspects qualify for the terming?

When exactly do literary theorists cease their labeling?

Why do critics cling on to age-old elements of literature?

Do writers dictate anything?

Neo-Romanticism

. . . birthed in the late 1930s and 1940s
by the imaginative and abstract paintings
of Paul Nash, Graham Sutherland and others . . .

birthing movements
in the fields of not only painting,
but also philosophy, literature, music, architecture,
and sociology . . .

The question now is:
What do we do with this piece of information?
Shall we train ourselves to obey by the prescribed rules
of the movement-labelers? Or . . .
Should we continue to write as our spirits guide us,
lead us, comfort us, embracing our particular path toward
creativity?

Have you settled down inside an answer yet?
Or . . . will you do as I do, and give no credence to
the so-called guidelines that are forced upon us
on an all-inclusive stage of universal literature?

Teresa E. Gallion

Teresa E. Gallion was born in Shreveport, Louisiana and moved to Illinois at the age of 15. She completed her undergraduate training at the University of Illinois Chicago and received her master's degree in Psychology from Bowling Green State University in Ohio. She retired from New Mexico state government in 2012.

She moved to New Mexico in 1987. While writing sporadically for many years, in 1998 she started reading her work in the local Albuquerque poetry community. She has been a featured reader at local coffee houses, bookstores, art galleries, museums, libraries, Outpost Performance Space, the Route 66 Festival in 2001 and the State of Oklahoma's Poetry Festival in Cheyenne, Oklahoma in 2004. She occasionally hosts an open mic.

Teresa's work is published in numerous Journals and anthologies. She has two CDs: *On the Wings of the Wind* and *Poems from Chasing Light.* She has published three books: *Walking Sacred Ground, Contemplation in the High Desert* and *Chasing Light.*

Chasing Light was a finalist in the 2013 New Mexico/Arizona Book Awards.

The surreal high desert landscape and her personal spiritual journey influence the writing of this Albuquerque poet. When she is not writing, she is committed to hiking the enchanted landscapes of New Mexico. You may preview her work at

http://bit.ly/1aIVPNq or ***http://bit.ly/13IMLGh***

Litany of a Hindi Writer

Chaturvedi, Indian poet, writer,
essayist, playwright and journalist.
Received many awards and honors
during his lifetime.

Remembered for participation in India's
struggle for independence.
Repeatedly incarcerated but continued
to speak and write against social evils
and in support of an equitable society.

Also known in the Neo-romanticism
movement of Hindi literature.
His writing leaned towards
themes of nationalist emotions,
love and nature.

Through the Maze

I step lightly on soft red sand,
sink deep in the dry beach,
glide in my imaginary boat.
I see ships of the desert
strolling on the horizon.

I want to chase their smiles.
Lines in the sand
shapeshift like a checker board.
I cannot see the best move
for a dysfunctional brain warp
holds my legs in check.

No running, no hiding.
Dragging my feet between
shadow and light.
The tunnel of desire
teases my taste buds.

And the ships of the desert
continue their slow burn north.
Perhaps they could distract me
from the maze of desire

that hangs over me
like a wedding veil.
An unwanted marriage of greed
nips at my ankles.

Release From the Wheel

My kisses ride in a boat
downstream to no ending.
A ripple rolls over your chest.

When I look at you,
your smile is like barbwire
waiting to shackle me.

I want to run but my legs refuse me.
I love too intensely.
Always caught in a slow burn.

I must learn the art of detachment
to rise from shackles
of grief and pain.

I do not want to engage anymore
mourners knocking at my door
to rug pain on my heart.

I grow tired of working the soil
and cuddle blistered hands
that scream for release
from the wheel of karma.

Ashok

K.

Bhargava

Ashok K. Bhargava

ASHOK BHARGAVA is a poet, writer, inspirational speaker and a literary consultant. He has attended poetry conferences in Italy, Turkey, India and Philippines. His latest book "Riding the Tide" about his battle with cancer has been translated and published in Arabic, Hindi, Telugu and Bengali languages. He is a contributing writer to several anthologies worldwide including World Poetry Almanac 2014. He has been published in numerous print and online magazines.

Ashok has won many accolades including Poet Ambassador to Japan, Kalidasa International award, World Poetry Lifetime Achievement award, Writers Beyond Borders Peace award and Tapsilog Leadership award for his community involvement. He is founder of Writers International Network Canada Society to discover, nourish, recognize and celebrate writers, poets and artists and to assist them to network with the community at large. He is the author of eight books of poetry and one anthology. He is Artist-in-Residence at Moberly Arts & Cultural Centre and also co-edits the literary section of The Link Newspaper.

Distraction or Denial: "A Flower's Wish"

To Makhanlal Chaturvedi

A flower that seems
uncertain,
where to land
as if it mattered.

If you ask me,
I think it is insincere
to call a senseless killing of a soldier
in a war, a deathtrap that leads
to nothingness,
a sacrifice or martyrdom
in the name of nationalism.

It is ignorance and
a denial of hope to view a life
to be cutoff in the apex of his youth,
glorified by the petals of flowers
scattered on the path of no return.

A Snub or Senility

It was 1990
when you were almost nine.
I walked
with my arm slung over your shoulders,
I loved doing that.

Remember,
I came home for you
almost every weekend
after 485 miles of drive.

You would wrap your arms around me
when I was to leave and say,
I want you to quit your job
and come back here.

Do you know
when it was the last time
you wrapped your arms
around someone's shoulder
and walked him home?

I love you but I don't know you
anymore.

New Season 2024

In the new
season of spring,
I feel new like
a delicate flower
a fresh bloom.

Green leaves youth
nascent,
true love budding branches,
welcome kiss,
lipstick pink
sky smiles.

I give you all,
my splendor
my fragrance
my seeds
my nectar
my moments of bliss.

Come on,
take it all
it is yours.

Caroline 'Ceri Naz' Nazareno Gabis

Caroline 'Ceri' Nazareno-Gabis

Caroline 'Ceri Naz' Nazareno-Gabis, author of Velvet Passions of Calibrated Quarks, World Poetry Canada International Director to Philippines is a multi-awarded poet, editor, journalist, educator, peace and women's advocate. She believes that learning other's language and culture is a doorway to wisdom.

Among her poetic belts include **Gabrielle Galloni Memorial Panorama International Youth Award** 2022, Panorama Youth Literary Awards 2020, 7th Prize Winner in the 19th, 20th and 21st Italian Award of Literary Festival; Writers International Network-Canada ''Amazing Poet 2015'', The Frang Bardhi Literary Prize 2014 (Albania), Poet Journalist Award 2014 (Tuzla, Istanbul, Turkey) and World Poetry Empowered Poet 2013 (Vancouver, Canada). She's a featured member of Association of Women's Rights and Development (AWID), The Poetry Posse, Galaktika Poetike, Asia Pacific Writers and Translators (APWT), Axlepino and Anacbanua. Her poetry and children's stories have been featured in different anthologies and magazines worldwide.

Links to her works:

http://panitikan.ph/2018/03/30/caroline-nazareno-gabis/

https://apwriters.org/author/ceri_naz/

http://www.aveviajera.org/nacionesunidasdelasletras/id1181.html

Selflessly, Chaturvedi

An Indian poet was born,
Makhanlal Chaturvedi, a name adorned,
Truth was his shield, words are his weapon,
Sinister reclaimed freedom for their own.
Very young teacher at sixteen, a journalist soon after,
His pen wrote for the rights of his people,
against the colonial chains,
He wrote with a fire that ran through his veins.
"Him Tarangini," his work, like the waves of the sea,
Chhayavaad's child, Neo-romanticism's star,
His poems spoke of the crowns of liberty,
both near and far.
"Pushp ki Abhilasha," a flower's desire,
A testament of his works on fire.
His words would dance,"Deep Se Deep Jale,"
Spreading hope and courage, tearing insentience
Makhanlal Chaturvedi, a name that inspires,
A poet, a patriot, whose spirit never tires.
His legacy breathes from morning to night,
His words are imprint of undying love!

Dawning Mercy

In the quiet of dawn, mercy whispers soft,

A gentle touch at all times,

It heals the broken hearts

A silent balm for the painful strife

A raindrop of mercy, a gentle perching bird

Giving hope, giving new life,

In its embrace, the world kneels

Pouring kind touches for the world that heals.

Written Wishes

I am penning down
My wishes upon the page,
I wish these words would dance in ink,
I wish Hope would fly before they shrink.
As a scribe of Love,
May these words touch your heart,
I wish Dreams would whisper in your stressful days,
May all the strengths in letter be uncurled,
Against the storms of doubt,
A testament to desire's demand,
Wishing the readers, that these simple words
Would kiss their hands in a wishful night,
The written word holds would light your way,
A beacon for the morrow's gaze, a resounding plea.

Swapna Behera

Swapna Behera

Swapna Behera is a trilingual poet, translator, environmentalist, editor from India and author of seven books of different genres including one on children's literature on Environment. She is the recipient of International UGADI AWARD 2019, honoured from Gujurat Sahitya Akademi 2022, 2021 International Poesis Award of Honor as Jury, Pentasi B World Fellow Poet, Honoured Poet of India from Seychelles Government and International awards from Algeria, Morocco, Kajhakhstan, modern Arabic Literary Renaissance of Egypt, International Arts Council Argentina etc. Her stories, poems, articles are published in many International and National magazines and ezines. Her poem A NIGHT IN THE REFUGEE CAMP is translated into 67 languages. She has received over 60 National and International Awards. At present she is the Cultural Ambassador for India and South Asia of Inner Child and the life member of Odisha Environmental Society

Email
swapna.behera@gmail.com

Web Site
http://swapnabehera.in/

Makhanlal Chaturvedi : a legacy of Neo Romanticism

a legacy
never stands
in the dark corner
it becomes
a flower ,
a tree ,
a soldier
a prisoner,
a youth,
a lover
a journalist
a bird
at time it cries
cries for the country
it smiles verses
climbs at towers
talks with the cuckoo
thinks of the
neoromanticism movement of literature
Him Kirtini, Him Tarangini
are your iconic creativity
you are a freedom fighter
pioneer of Neo romanticism
a humble teacher at the age of sixteen
a trend setter is seldom born
you deserve all reverence
you are a legacy
as you know the strength of alphabets

the wooden door travels

shukrana

the wooden door is reaching me today
travelling two countries
I am in one country
my brothers in my neighbouring country
I was a professor there once upon a time
my family left our land , shop ,the street
where we brothers played ,learnt to ride bicycle
enjoyed jaggery sweets ,its fragrances
throughout the years the delicacies from sugar cane juice
our tractors in the wheat field
we grow with the trees harvesting corn
the cow dung fire and common cooking in the courtyard
ladies sing songs,
girls having long plaits dazzled with bright red ribbon
evening tea time we discuss politics to farming
enjoying the smell of the boiled corns and semolina made
from fathomed buffalo milk
together we grow with animals ,flowers in a joint family
one midnight every thing changed
two countries sang two different national anthems under
two flags
everything is divided
people travelled sitting on train roofs,
millions died
can our tears travel?
my father stayed there
mother here
children missed the collective songs ,the streets, the foot
ball fields
today our grand children understand the pain of tears
pain of migration

today my friend had sent the door of my old house
where the finger prints of my ancestors are engraved
I have cataract; cannot see the antique door
but can feel my granny, can listen the sound of the court yard
the door with the legal documents is travelling to me alone
with the valid stamp marks of two countries
the price of Independence is too expensive
the lost memories are affluent
certainly, the tears tear hearts and souls
I am a retired professor
waiting to receive the door of our house
with the hall marks of my ancestors
dear grandson of my brother
thanks a lot for this precious gift
should I celebrate or cry
I am confused …
a paradise is lost or found
I wish to feel the heartbeat of the door

(shukrana :- thanks)

mists are hanging

seasons collapse
no one listens
look at the ocean
hold your tongue
there is a light house
search your vision
the sketchy skeleton
searching for a land to grow rice
the clocks melt
nepotism ,nihilism, despotism
and
all isms are in search of peace
there is a holocaust
and cacophony
what about the rights of
the birds and animals
do something
the clones are chirping
AI teachers can teach
the veins and arteries
we will miss the great
story tellers and love makers
artists will peep
to draw the lines or circles
who intrigued us?
mists are hanging …….

Albert 'Infinite' Carrasco

Albert 'Infinite' Carassco

Albert "Infinite The Poet" Carrasco is an urban poet, mentor and public speaker.

Albert believes his experience of growing up in poverty, dealing with drugs and witnessing murder over and over were lessons learnt, in order to gain knowledge to teach. Albert's harsh reality and honesty is a powerfully packed punch delivered through rhyme. Infinite grew up in the east part of the Bronx and still resides there, so he knows many young men will follow the same dark path he followed looking for change. The life of crime should never be an option to being poor but it is, very often.

Infinite poetry @lulu.com

Alcarrasco2 on YouTube

Infinite the poet on reverbnation

Infinite Poetry

www.lulu.com/us/en/shop/al-infinite-carrasco/infinite-poetry/paperback/product-21040240.html

www.innerchildpress.com/albert-carrasco

Makhanlal Chaturvedi

He was born in Babai, India, he was an intelligent kid, at sixteen he became a teacher.
He was a poet, writer, essayist, playwright and a journalist all put together.
He'll will infinitely be known for his contribution to Chhayavaad, Hindu literature.
Prison couldn't stop him during the British raj,
all that did was give him more time to become a deeper thinker,
to disburse his words in a poetic barrage.
He had one job, and that was to stand ten toes down for his people,
by speaking and writing against social evils.
An equitable and exploration - free society,
was a shared vision between him and Mahatma Gandhi
Moving in his own lane and accord,
made him stand out from the rest and earn many awards.
The Madura Pradesh cultural council,
hosted annual Samaroh because he was so influential.

The traditional curse

I remember hearing the sounds of joy and laughter then looking out the window and seeing my peers enjoying a simple life, I wanted to be out there with them too, but I had things to do, like get back to the stove and finishing up the whipping process that was in progress before I walked to the window with butta residue on my butter knife.

I quickly went from a boy to man trying to stack racks from a thousand grams to help the fam. I promised to step up when I was leaving the cemetery telln dad to rest up. I did, I was surrounded by drug dealers tryn to make it big, killers fresh home from bids, dope fiends, coke hitters and those that burned glass to beam.

This would be my environment and lifestyle for a long time, I broke night after night dealing with long lines for nickel and dime white crime. In those broken nights many men saw the light before reachn the end of the tunnel, I'm not talkn bout accomplishments or goals I'm talking bout the light from barrels before slugs make bodies cold.

It was a lucrative but deadly path, there was no fork in the road, it was either stay poor or navigate through the garden of hell where the seeds that sprout the red root of evil are planted to make some rich and others maggot food or ash. A lot of bodies decomposed in caskets and were placed in urns ending their run, without a question more souls got closer to the sun than those that made it in the slums

Bike Life

I'll wake up early take care of my hygiene then throw on timbs, a long sleeve and jeans. I'll grab my gloves and specs ready to catch reck. Mom duke be riffn because my apartment smelled like oil on the days I left my bike in the jects. I'll pull it out and take it down in the elevator in a wheelie, walk it out the lobby, start the YZ and let it rev a little while blazn Marley. As soon as it's done, I'll spin the block meltn knobbies waitn to meet up with the rest of my Castle Hill dirt bike riders so we could do our Soundview trails, Ferry Point or BX to Harlem runs. In a few minutes there's kX's CR's and RM's buzzn thru the slums. We didn't have to call each other, who ever heard the one down and five up sounds, if they had the "fever" they immediately came down. We'll buzz to Soundview and wait for everyone to come out on cozy, we'll go to Monroe and waited for them boys on story then we headed to Watson, they had a crazy crew throw'n up the east coast W, now there's bikes, banshees and pilots too. From there we decided if we was going to hit the dirt or pavement

Michelle
Joan
Barulich

Michelle Joan Barulich

Michelle Joan Barulich was born in Honolulu, Hawaii on the island of Oahu. She started writing poetry and songs with her younger brother Paul. They have written many songs in their teen years. She is currently studying Alternative Medicine and would like to become a Homeopathic Doctor. Michelle loves all kinds of animals and birds; she does wild rehabilitation. She has also rescued rock pigeons that make great pets.

https://www.facebook.com/michelle.barulich

Makhanlal

In the realm of literature
You are a renowned poet, writer, and journalist
You were the first of its kind
In the whole world of Asia
You used your writing to persuade the Indian masses
To protect against the British regime
You also received the annual
"Makhanlal Chaturvedi" for excellence in poetry
by an Indian poet
You will always have a lasting legacy.

Unspoken Words

Sad songs that I listen to
Funny how I think of you
Before you left there was so many words
You wanted to say
But no one would listen
There was so many feelings
You wanted to touch
But no one could care that much
I hear my crying out loud
Each tear means something to me
And if the light of the dawn breaks first
Will you still leave
With unspoken words unleft to say?
I can hear voices in your head
There calling your name
I can come in touch with your fears
I can retrace yesterday's heartaches
For I understand
There was so many unspoken words
To be revealed, now they lye in the dead...

The Girl Who Stands Alone

Out from the darkness
Out from the cold
Her life is hell
A battle to overcome
Victory is accounting the tears she has shed
Walking into crowds of unknown
People sip their wine without recognizing
Though you don't know her, your mind is recalling
In the depth of time
Planned beforehand, she conserved herself for you
Then hoping in her sadness shame
It was just as it was
She waited like the last time
Believing you would not go that far
That time was wrong
You see, she's the girl who stands alone
Disguising her hurt, crying all alone
And if she cannot speak a line
Will you just walk on by?
Leaving her behind, to break her once more inside
She blushes in the silent room
The clock bangs, and beats the hours
Another chapter reveals her darkness
Her golden green eyes see right through you
Reading every feeling that you feel
But can you understand what she's going through?
Or is your judgement the fatalism of her?
She's the girl who stands alone
Killing her inside, but she won't let it show
There is no accounting then for my regret
That you were someone else's
And if I smile, I can say knowing that somewhere you

believed me
Only an empty shadow knows
There is no accounting then for my request
That you were someone else's
I cannot forget and I can say
Knowing that somewhere you believed me
Once is for all time
You see, she's the girl who stands alone
Separated from the rest
Facing the world on her own
Yes, she's the one, the girl who stands alone...

Eliza Segiet

Eliza Segiet graduated with a Master's Degree in Philosophy at Jagiellonian University.

Received *Global Literature Guardian Award* – from Motivational Strips, World Nations Writers Union and Union Hispanomundial De Escritores (UHE) 2018.

Nominated for the Pushcart Prize 2019, 2021.

Laureate *Naji Naaman Literary Prize 2020*,

International Award Paragon of Hope (2020),

World Award 2020 *Cesar Vallejo* for Literary Excellence. Laureate of the Special Jury *Sahitto International Award* 2021, World Award *Premiul Fănuș Neagu* 2021.

Finalist *Golden Aster Book* World Literary Prize 2020, *Mili Dueli* 2022, Voci nel deserto 2022.

At the international Festival of Poetry CAMPIONATO MONDIALE DI POESIA (2021/2022) she won the title of vice-champion of the world.

Award BHARAT RATNA RABINDRANATH TAGORE INTERNATIONAL AWARD (2022).

Award - *World Poets Association* (2023).

Laureate Between words and infinity *"International Literary Award (2023).*

Spark

*In memory of Makhanlal Chaturvedi**

National sentiments
were for him
an igniting spark
to fight against the social evil.

Love and respect for his country
drove him to fight for independence;
– his sword – poetry
– his floret – verbal ability to capture people.
In his verses
he sketched their hopes –

– freedom for the
fatherland, even at the cost of one's life.

**A poem dedicated to Pandit Makhanlal Chaturvedi, an Indian poet, writer, and journalist, remembered for his contribution to India's struggle for independence.*

Translated by Dorota Stępińska

Sense

Watch out!
It can happen at any time.
You must be alert,
it may come from an unexpected side.

It will try to pull you towards itself.
Don't ask yourself if it makes sense!
Or if it is worth the trouble.

Let it happen. Let yourself be seduced.
It's always better to be loved
than to always yearn for imaginary one.
It is not a naked body
that can awaken your senses –
only goodness has such power.

The most valuable are the days
– not the nights.
These are short.
When the day comes,
it's important
to have something to talk about to each ot.

The longed for, the expected,
the desired one,
comes unexpectedly.
When it happens,
the previously fading silence of the heart
may blaze with heat!

Translated by Dorota Stępińska

Barrier

An easily passable corridor
divided their vivid desires
– her embarrassed
– him shy.

These two
– insurmountable -
meters were
– respect barrier
– doubt.

A wall cemented
with heart and mind,

too high,
to carve a little delight.

In the morning they whispered,
that one day, that maybe together...

That perhaps...

this unfulfillment
was to kill the myth.

Translated by Dorota Stępińska

William S. Peters Sr.

William S. Peters, Sr.

Bill's writing career spans a period of well over 50 years. Being first Published in 1972, Bill has since went on to Author in excess of 50+ additional Volumes of Poetry, Short Stories, etc., expressing his thoughts on matters of the Heart, Spirit, Consciousness and Humanity. His primary focus is that of Love, Peace and Understanding!

Bill says . . .

I have always likened Life to that of a Garden. So, for me, Life is simply about the Seeds we Sow and Nourish. All things we "Think and Do", will "Be" Cause and eventually manifest itself to being an "Effect" within our own personal "Existences" and "Experiences" . . . whether it be Fruit, Flowers, Weeds or Barren Landscapes! Bill highly regards the Fruits of his Labor and wishes that everyone would thus go on to plant "Lovely" Seeds on "Good Ground" in their own Gardens of Life!

to connect with Bill, he is all things Inner Child

www.iaminnerchild.com

Personal Web Site

www.iamjustbill.com

The Spirit Speaks

I am but a 'Freedom Fighter'
Championing the rights of sovereignty.

I stand not alone
In this wilderness
Offering to the heavens
My thoughts, my words, my poems and my prose
Telling the story
Characterizing our plight,
Your plight
To our world

I am a rebel they say,
I say I am but a man
Whose spirit is troubled
By the times
We are given to endure

O dear 'Liberation',
Come unto to my people
And lift this oppressive hand
From our shoulders . . .

Let us find 'Righteousness'
Let us all collect, come together
For the good of one,
The good of all

May who I am
Be embraced by the heavens
And my offerings
Be a beacon of light

In this darkness,
And rise up, rise up
And shower themselves
The blessings of compassion
Upon the world of us all

the Garden of Even

there once was a Village
that had a Garden
where nothing but Love ever grew
the Fruits were Divine
what was mine was thine
this was what everyone knew

and then came a thought
which some sadly bought
that i was different from you
and to all of dismay
came forth the day
when this paradigm then became true

the children were confused
and some were used
to further the separation of self
and some gathered night
and held on quite tight
for they thought that things were wealth

and as time went on
the old life was gone
where they all lived simply as one
and wouldn't you know
even their personal glow
was fading and almost done

but much to their mirth
the Mother called Earth
gave an awakening call
it was not for the few
but all that She knew
she called before the fall

now some did transcend
before the end
of this fictional story i tell
but within every myth
there is a sweet gift
that each may come and dispel

so please come on back home
to the garden you're from
where all is balanced and square
the Garden of Even
where there is no needin'
for love indwells everywhere

We do what we can

We may not be the strongest,
The smartest,
The most able
Or most stable, but
We do what we can,
Don't we

Life challenges us
To become bigger and faster,
And at other times
Slower and smaller.
I am not sure about
The shorter or the taller,
But that does not negate
The dichotomous nature
Of our existence, does it?

We are up, we are down,
Over and over again

Gaining new friends,
Losing old ones
Due to politics, opinions, geography
And death.

Perhaps life is like that proverbial onion
And we keep peeling the skin away
Layer by layer
Until we get to something usable
Or nothing at all
While the tears
Continue to fall

Some search and seek earnestly
For fame and fortune,
While others are never noticed
By notoriety

Some are content
For what they have,
For in their estimation
They have enough....
While others will never
Get to enjoy
That sweet respite

Some like to invade
The halls of solace
With their noisysome presence
Never to care
Who the may disturb or offend.
And then there are those
Who walk in humble humility
With little or no aspirations
To leave footprints,
In the garden
Or pluck the petals
Off the flowers of life

Some seek the light,
Some find comfort
In the shadows.
Some speak loudly,
Some voices are softly given.
Some could never be quiet,
And speak with excess,
While others are satisfied
With their inner thinking,
And the peace it affords.

Some smile,
Some frown,
Some are stoic.

Some play,
Some work,
All in varying degrees.
Some are minimalist,
Some are excessive.

Some dance,
Some paint flowers on the wall
And others are the ones
Who play the music
.....
Me, I love to observe

I believe
There is an earnestly we all have
To live our lives
In our own way
Even if 'that way'
Has been adopted from others,
Be they weak,
Be they strong,
Be they smart, able or stable,
Or not...

But, when it is all said and done . ..
Each man, each woman ....
We do what we can.

May
2024
Featured Poets

Binod Dawadi

Petros Kyriakou Veloudas

Rayees Ahmad Kumar

Solomon C Jatta

i
Fly
because
I Can
. . . said the Dreamer to the world.
www.iamjustbill.com

Binod Dawadi

Binod Dawadi

Binod Dawadi, the author of The Power of Words, is a master's degree holder in Major English. He has worked on more than 1000 anthologies published in various renowned magazines. His vision is to change society through knowledge, so he wants to provide enlightenment to the people through his writing skills.

God

Where are you God ?
I am in a pains,
I am in a trouble,
I need your love,
As well as your help,
Who else can love as well as,
Help me in this materialistic and selfish world,
Give me some powers,

As well as strength to work,
Make my destiny,
Give me some good luck,
Uplift my life,
From your blessings,
My God,
I am searching you,
And feeling you at everything.

False Love

Don't come in my life,
Don't show me,
Your false love,
I couldn't give you anything,
I am poor man,
Instead obstacles and pains,
You couldn't accept anything from me,
So, you can't give me,

Your true and spiritual love,
So go away from me,
I don't want your false love,
In my life,
May be you have shown dreams,
To many as well as,
Destroyed their life,
But please don't destroy my life.

Imagination Of Magic

I see in the sky,
And in ground,
If I could get some invisible,
Powers and magic,
If I could change a brick to a gold,
And become rich,
I could fulfill my dreams,
As well as of the poor,

People of the world,
I will rub their tears,
Treat their diseases,
As well as give them a new life,
No orphans will be there,
No poor people will be there,
I could do this,
If I get some powers and some magic inside me.

Petros
Kyriakou
Veloudas

Petros Kyriakou Veloudas was born in Agrinio in 1977. He has a degree in humanities from the Department of Hellenic Culture of the Hellenic Open University of Patras, works as a private employee and is also a preschool teacher and radio producer. He is a European ambassador of Greek poetry in Romania, an academic poet at the AMCL poetry and philology academy in Brazil. Member of the international poetry societies WORLD SOCIETY OF POETS-WSP, UNION OF WRITERS, International Society of Greek Writers-DEEL.

His literary-poetic work is included in the Great Encyclopedia of Contemporary Greek Writers CHARI PATSI., as well as in numerous anthologies of Greek and international poetry, he has won 57 international poetry prizes and his poems have been translated into numerous languages. have been published in local newspapers of Agrinio such as (MACHITIS, ANANGELIA, PALMOS).

The Honey of Poetry"

I know these steps are
your thoughts that bored
crawling, supported
from the feelings of passion…
They take slow, torturous steps until
to arrive at a poem and
comfortable to sit
on the armchair
of the rhymes of…
Then the inspiration
sleepy, drowsy
in ink wrinkles
as if beaten
in person
cancer rapping
nods her head
pillow,
bench not to
eat standing
the lyrics
At midnight.
The pen signs
in the body of inspiration
the initials of a pain
reflection...
Suddenly the old hand of inspiration
now he holds the bloody one tighter
pen giving the myth the pen
to tattoo her a feather
white horse called Pegasus...
This demon horse is chasing a
wild bee flying from a flower
in flower of verses gathering
finally, all delicious
honey of irresistible ...poetry!

Poem Written With The Pen Of The Soul"

He lives by walking
on a taut rope
compromise repressed
Take good care
and it doesn't slip
not even in the shadows
of his fears..
At the bottom of the tunnel
his eyes become
sparkling
moons of high brightness
Meet in the dark
the Apology
an apparition with
dusty clothes,
messy white hair
gives him a steal
kiss
on the cheek
and...disappears!..
in the body of a ...cloud
He's moving on
towards the exit of the wrinkled
tunnel
there she welcomes him
blue-eyed Kindness,
Blonde Hair
and a sun once
for his hat he holds
hand tenderly
and gives him a flower

rose
heart shaped
He missed that
a pure heart
to wipe him
his tears
from the ...clouds
of his ..soul!

Dinner with Phobias

To visit
his fears
is his qualification
of his own inner self...
To flourish the social
his phobias invite them
in his modest living room,
speaks loudly to them,
raps them and
then like a white dove,
the wings open to shine
their pains…
That's how you hurt me too
he says to his phobias
he raises his glass high in a toast with
brusquely full
wine of emotions
and with his fears
becomes a romantic ….couple
He now feels detached,
free
to breathe
to reflect...
Every fear one
little quarrel
on the shores of the soul
Is it called fear?
human coexistence
dubious to a Platonist
love body?
Love makes everything beautiful
and tenderly soothes their fears!

Rayees
Ahmad
Kumar

Rayees Ahmad Kumar

Rayees Ahmad Kumar Is a columnist hailing from Qazigund Kashmir India. He is an academician, poet, Fiction Writer and his columns appear regularly in valley based major English and Urdu dailies, weeklies and monthly magazines.

Autumn

The dancing fall of dry withered leaves
Golden floor under the Chinar trees
Cool and refreshing breeze of morns and eves
Harvesting of paddy in the fields
Picking of apples and other fruits
Stored in the wicker baskets
Men women equally busy in lands
Lunch for the men, women carry
In wicker baskets on their heads
Threshing of walnuts a usual scene
Children preparing for their exams
Hide and seek of the electricity
Annoy students and displease others
Ladies burn drywood to make charcoal
Used during winter in the fire-pots
Sundrying the vegetables in wicker baskets
Which during harsh winter are cooked
To get a break from the busy work
Workers smoke through traditional Hubble-Bubble
Sometimes when it rains suddenly
People rush to protect their crops
Young working class of villages
Prepare to leave for outside the valley
Where they earn livelihood
And protect themselves from the biting cold
Like the pleasant spring season
Autumn in valley too is mesmerizing.

Winter woes

Vallities proudly during summers
Look forward to construct lofty
And cemented concrete houses
From its entrance to the top
Cement and marble flooring
Add to its resplendence and glory
In our strides, we only intend
To have charming, nice-looking house
We do forget it all about
The bone-chilling and biting cold
Of valley's tough and harsh winter
When faucets pour ice in place of water
Frozen metallic pipes burst
Amidst record dipping mercury levels
Our limbs experiencing osteodynia
Cracked-heals and chapped lips
Do annoy and infuriate us ponderously
During frequent power outages
All electrical gadgets stored in the home
Deny to provide any relief and comfort
In such testing and troubled times
Our traditional centuries old Kangri
Only comes to our rescue
Inhabitants in winters do acknowledge
The momentousness of muddy houses
With thatched roofs and timber-frames
And pitfalls of erecting concrete edifices.

Dejectedness

In this vast but finite world
While traversing on the vehicle of life
My eyes have deeply beholden, that
Someone dwells as if in heaven.

Worldly comforts and luxuries
Natural elegance of the planet
Varied flora and fauna of globe
Innumerable colourful flowers
Infinite multicolored chirping birds
Do please him, lessen his melancholy
And make an end of his gloom.

But for an unlucky and ill-fated one
All these sources of -
Bliss, comfort, tranquility, and contentment
Are trifling, tawdry, grimcrack, trashy and shoddy.

As he is ill-treated, tormented, brutalized
Agonized, victimized and mishandled
Within his own four walls
By his kinsfolk, consanguinean and flesh
For whom he spends sleepless nights
Toils hard through arduous paths
And himself lives miserably and austerilly.

Solomon C. Jatta

Solomon C. Jatta

Solomon C Jatta is a Gambian Lawyer and a poet whose literally work focuses on issues affecting his society and humanity. His works focus on love, social justice, and the need for change in Africa.

Wolves

Wolves, they come dressed like sheep,
Their kin fly with the bird, the masses to take boats of eternal sleep.
"Saviors of the people" only to fill their pocket,
Milking dry the collective bucket.

Critics of the crown silenced by positions.
Their speeches at war with their actions,
They command war while they run for peace,
Leaving the states restless while they lie in heavenly ease.

Here politics lack integrity and shame,
Seeking only fame and who to blame.
Principles and virtues they preach
Forgetting all when position they reach.

Holding The Sun

If you want it stretch your hand,
Nothing done can't give you something.
The sun isn't too far that you cannot hold,
You only dream because it is possible.
The moon maybe too far away
But it isn't beyond your reach.
If you too eager for fun,
Run not after it until you are rich.
If you want the crown,
You only gain through a walk in the thorn.
You want heaven, earth must be your hell,
The world wasn't made to be easy
Nor is it for the lazy, so be busy.

Burial At Sea

Three hours pass midnight we set sail,
Darkness the cover to help avoid any trail
Of the Navy that hunts us down.
We've heard of tales of men drown,
But we had hope of sailing through hell to get to heaven.
But all we see here is endless deep ocean raving
With madness. All we hear, the deafening sound of the Yamaha wailing
As if mourning our dead that lurks behind tall tides eager for killing.
The journey was to last for a week
But the wait is forever, leaving us weak.
Men fell sick, vomiting and thirsty but only salty water to quench our thirst.
None wished to die first
For all that died there wasn't a proper funeral.
Here there isn't a burial,
No sand to dig, nor the fires to cremate,
So in the deep sea we discarded all our good mate.

Remembering

our fallen soldiers of verse

Janet Perkins Caldwell

February 14, 1959 ~ September 20, 2016

Alan W. Jankowski

16 March 1961 ~ 10 March 2017

The Butterfly Effect

"IS" in effect

Inner Child Press

News

Published Books

by

Poetry Posse Members

We are so excited to share and announce a few of the current books, as well as the new and upcoming books of some of our Poetry Posse authors.

On the following pages we present to you ...

Alicja Maria Kuberska

Jackie Davis Allen

Gail Weston Shazor

hülya n. yılmaz

Nizar Sartawi

Elizabeth E. Castillo

Faleeha Hassan

Fahredin Shehu

Kimberly Burnham

Caroline 'Ceri' Nazareno

Eliza Segiet

Teresa E. Gallion

William S. Peters, Sr.

Now Available

www.innerchildpress.com

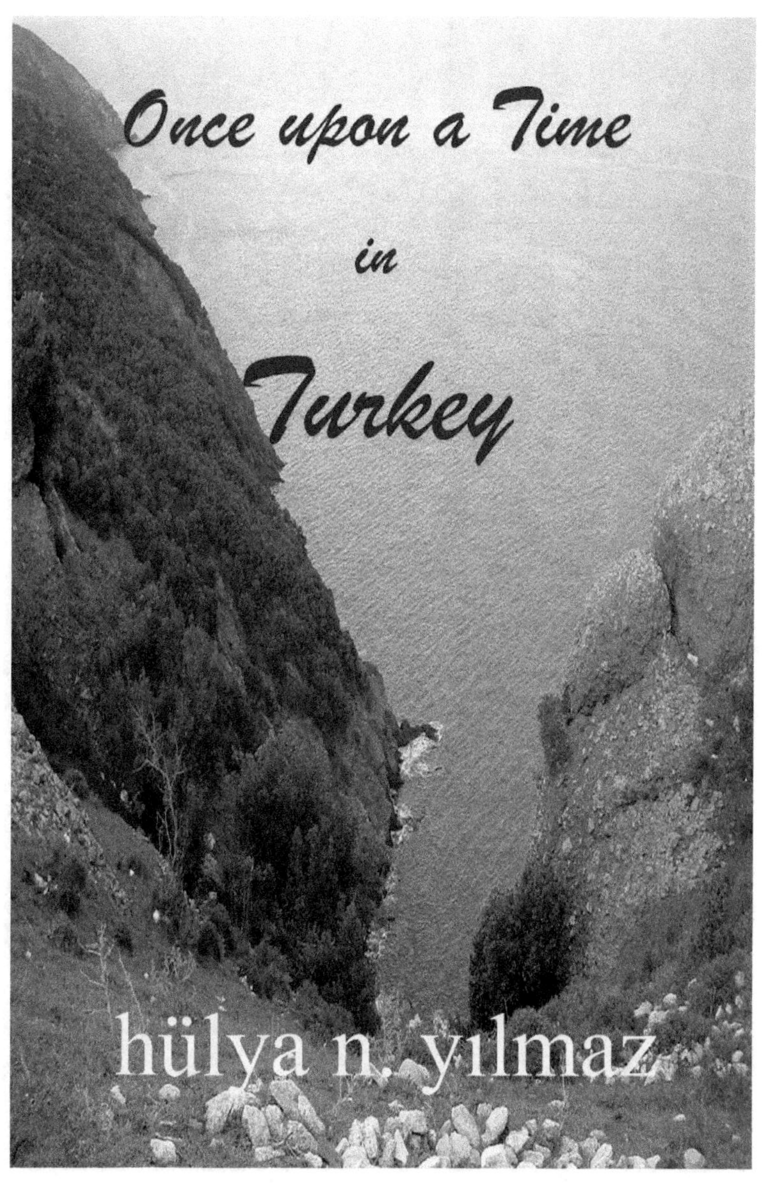
Once upon a Time
in
Turkey
hülya n. yılmaz

Unapologetically
BLACK
&
Blues
william s. peters, sr.

Now Available

www.innerchildpress.com

Pulling Coats
Shareef Abdur-Rasheed

Now Available

www.innerchildpress.com

UMAMI
The Essence of Deliciousness
Fahredin Shehu

Now Available

www.innerchildpress.com

After the Frost
Alicja Maria Kuberska

Now Available

www.innerchildpress.com

Fahredin Shehu
ORMUS

Now Available

www.innerchildpress.com

Ahead of My Time
. . . from the Streets to the Stages
Albert 'Infinite' Carrasco

Now Available

www.innerchildpress.com

Eliza Segiet
To Be More

Now Available at

www.amazon.com/gp/product/B08MYL5B7S/ref=dbs_a_def_rwt_hsch_vapi_tkin_p1_i2

SEARCH FOR THE MAGICAL MULTILINGUAL FROG
A Tale of Ribbit in 50 Languages
KIMBERLY BURNHAM

Now Available at

www.innerchildpress.com

Scent of Love
Poetry by
Teresa E. Gallion

Now Available

www.innerchildpress.com

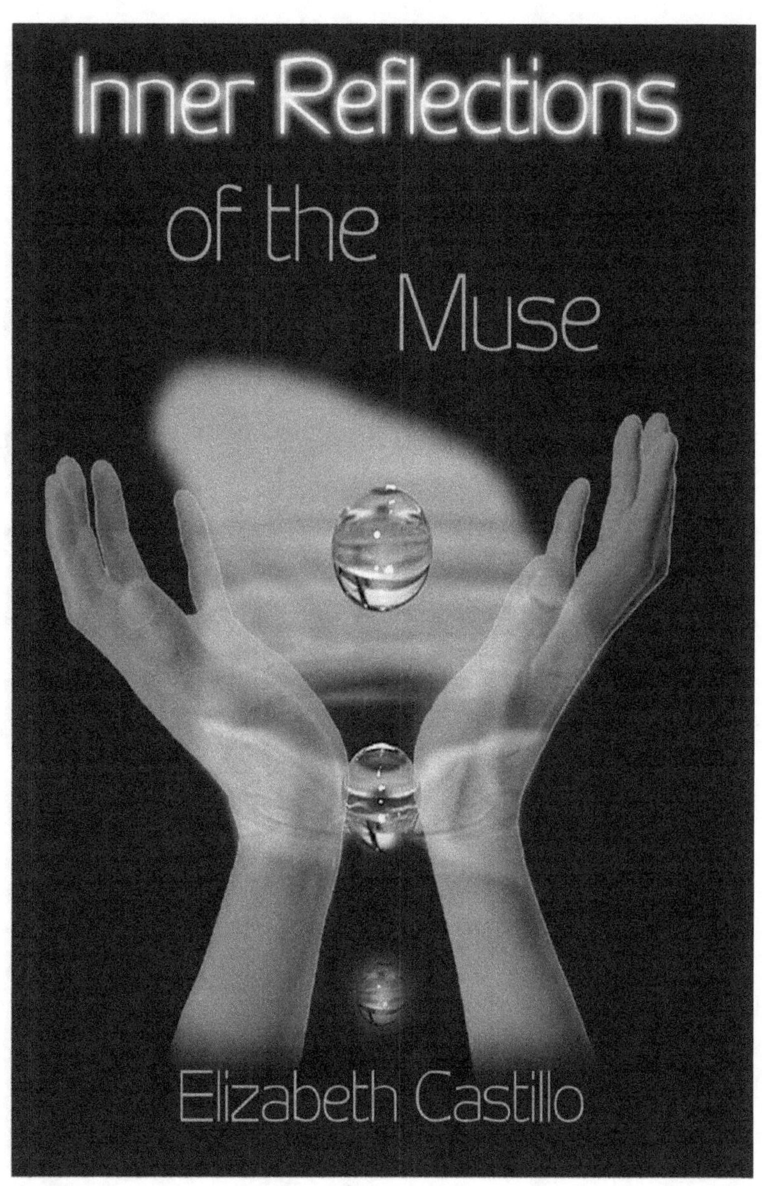
Inner Reflections
of the
Muse
Elizabeth Castillo

Now Available

www.innerchildpress.com

Letter - Poems
from a Beloved
hülya n. yılmaz

Now Available

www.innerchildpress.com

The
Utah
Chronicles
William S. Peters, Sr.

One Eye Open
unir1.
william s. peters, sr

Now Available

www.innerchildpress.com

The Book of krisar
volume v
william s. peters, sr.

The Book of krisar

Volume I
william s. peters, sr.

The Book of krisar

Volume II

william s. peters, sr.

Now Available

www.innerchildpress.com

Velvet Passions
of
Calibrated Quarks
Caroline Nazareno-Gabis

Now Available

www.innerchildpress.com

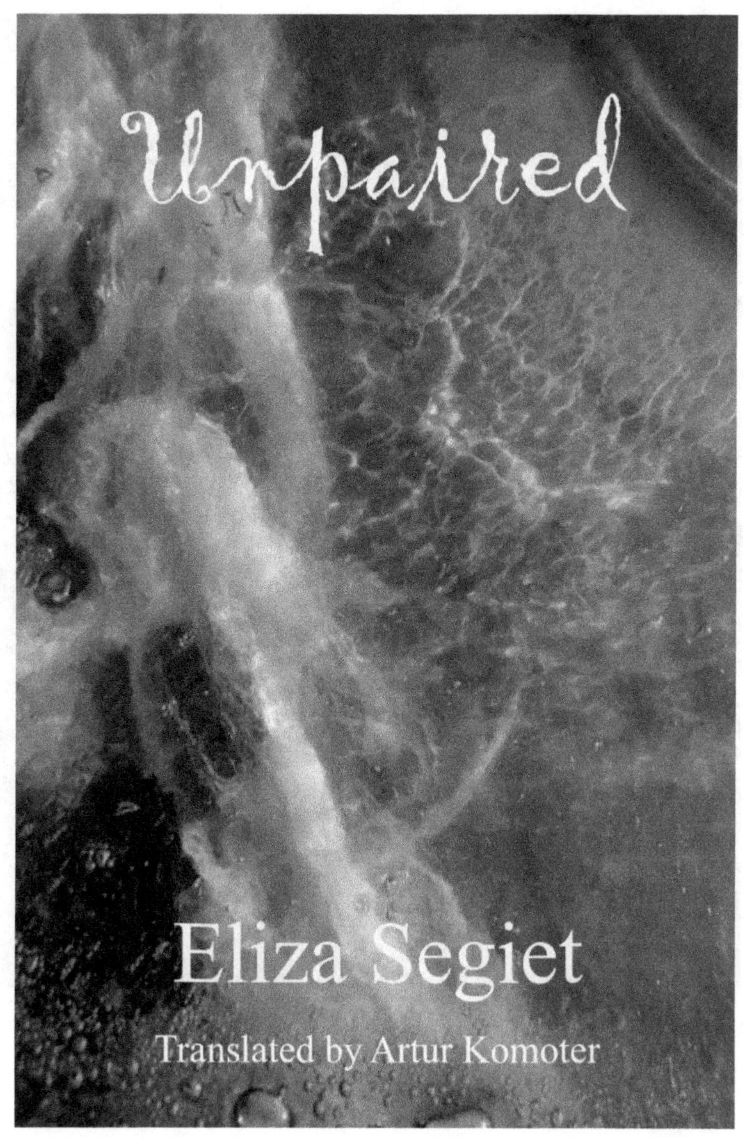
Unpaired
Eliza Segiet
Translated by Artur Komoter

Private Issue

www.innerchildpress.com

Canlarım
My Lifeblood
poetry in Turkish and English
hülya n. yılmaz

Butterfly's Voice
Faleeha Hassan
Translated by William M. Hutchins

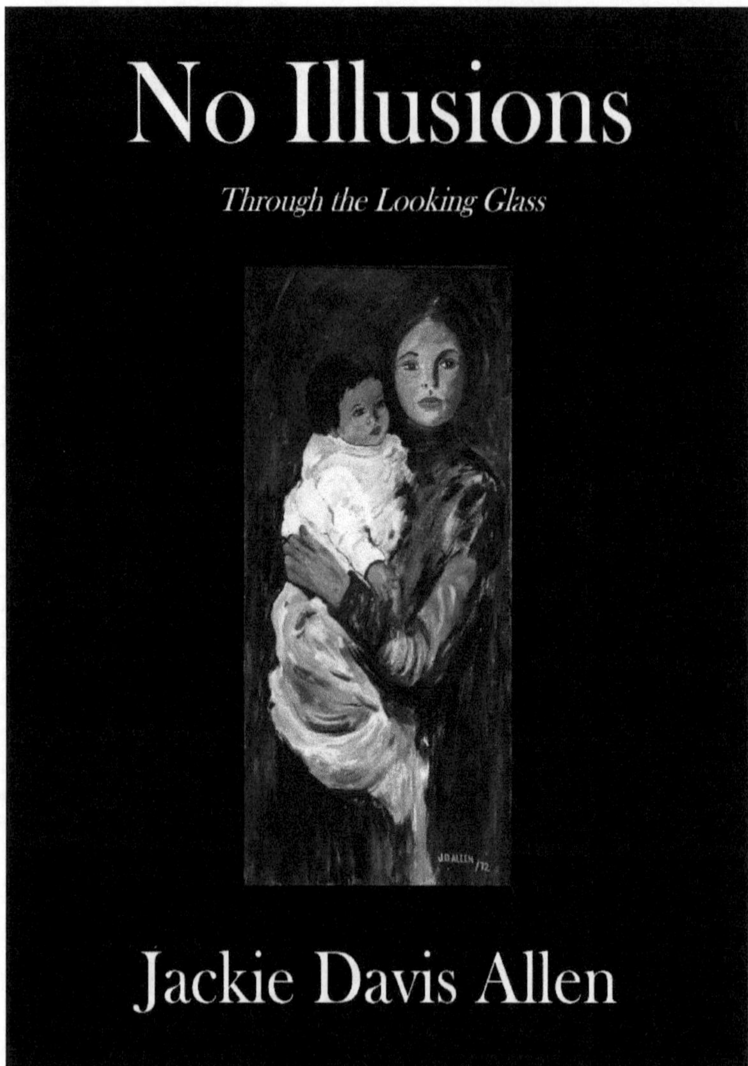
No Illusions
Through the Looking Glass
Jackie Davis Allen

Now Available at

www.innerchildpress.com

this and that
a hodge-podge of hülya's … poetry
hülya n. yılmaz

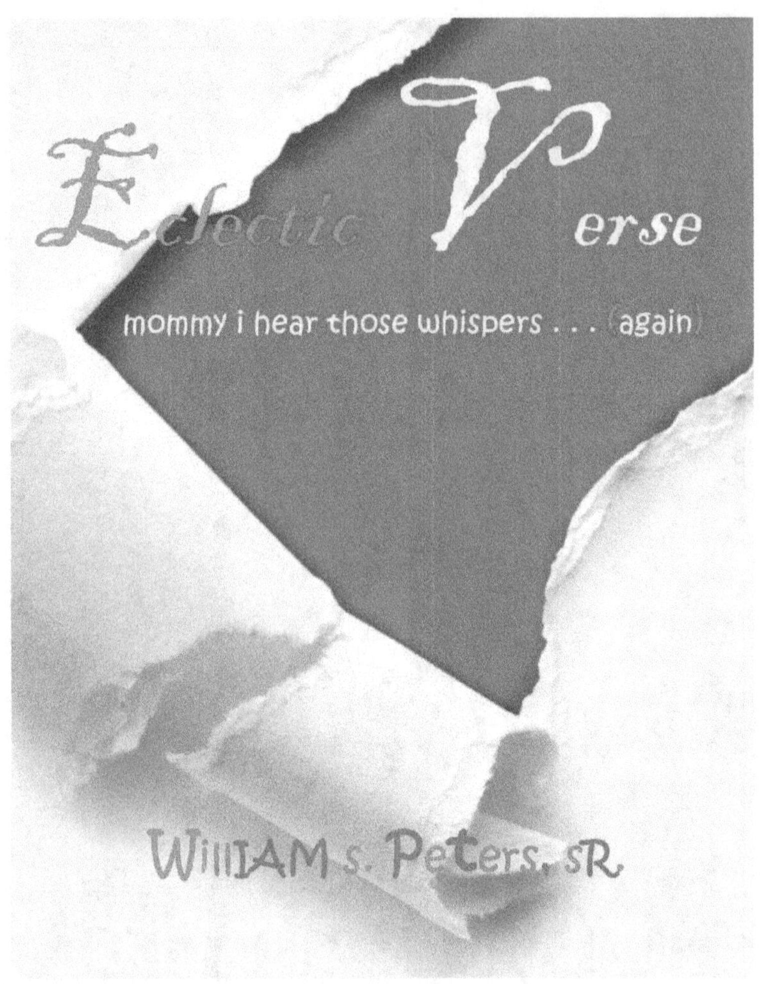
Eclectic Verse
mommy i hear those whispers . . . (again)
WillIAM s. Peters, sR

HERENOW

FAHREDIN SHEHU

Magnetic People
Eliza Segiet
Translated by Artur Komoter

Now Available at

www.innerchildpress.com

Dark Side
of the
Moon
Jackie Davis Allen

Now Available at

www.innerchildpress.com

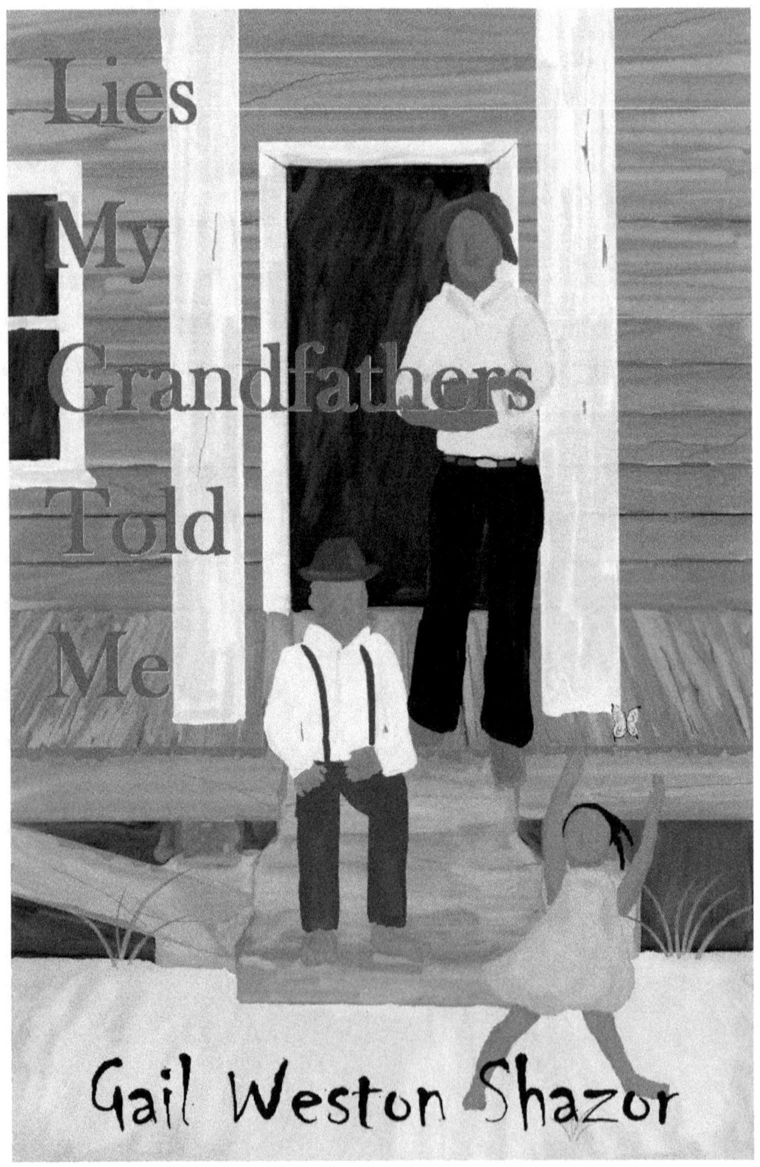
Lies
My
Grandfathers
Told
Me
Gail Weston Shazor

Now Available at

www.innerchildpress.com

Aflame
Memoirs in Verse
hülya n. yılmaz

Mass Graves
Faleeha Hassan

Now Available at

www.innerchildpress.com

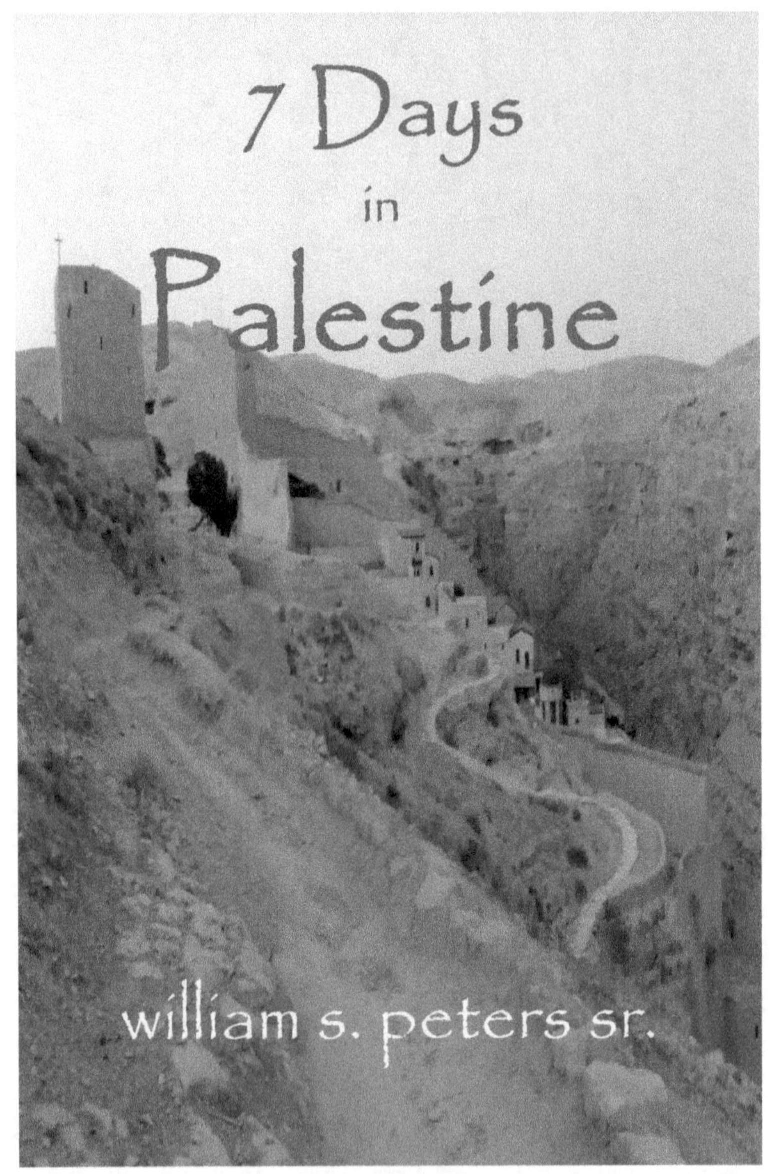
7 Days
in
Palestine
william s. peters sr.

Now Available at

www.innerchildpress.com

inner child press
presents
Tunisian Dreams
william s. peters, sr.

Now Available at

www.innerchildpress.com

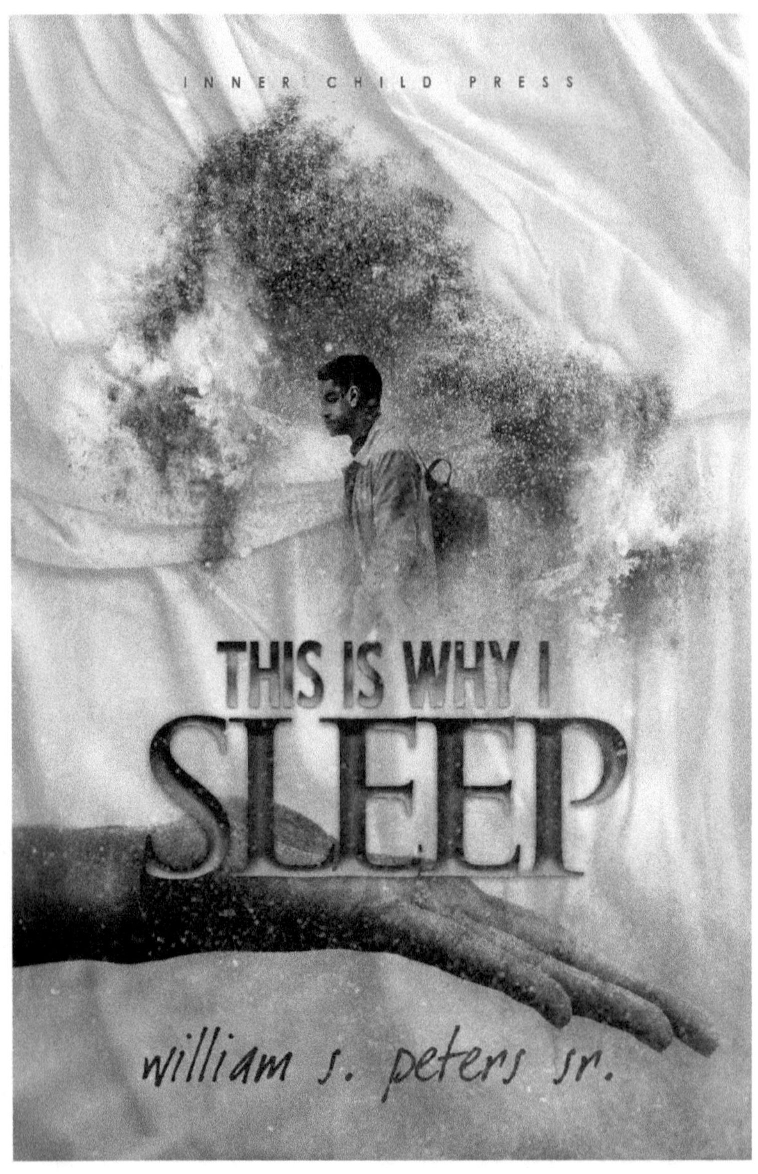
INNER CHILD PRESS
THIS IS WHY I
SLEEP
william s. peters sr.

Inward Reflections
This could work...
Yes...
I got it...
Ohh...
Think on These Things
Book II
william s. peters, sr.

Other

Anthological

works from

Inner Child Press International

www.innerchildpress.com

Inner Child Press
presents
WORLD HEALING
WORLD PEACE
2024
Poets for Humanity

Now Available

www.worldhealingworldpeacepoetry.com

World Healing
World Peace
2022
Poets for Humanity

Now Available

www.worldhealingworldpeacepoetry.com

World Healing World Peace
2020
Poets for Humanity

Now Available

www.worldhealingworldpeacepoetry.com

I Want To
Live
an examination of Black & White issues
Poetry
Analyses
Stories
Creative
Writing
Critical essays
Writers for Humanity

Now Available

www.innerchildpress.com

Inner Child Press International
&
The Year of the Poet
present

Poetry

the best of 2020

Poets of the World

Now Available
www.innerchildpress.com

Inner Child Press International
presents
W.A.R.
We Are Revolution
Poets for Humanity

the Heart of a Poet
words for a better tomorrow
The Conscious Poets

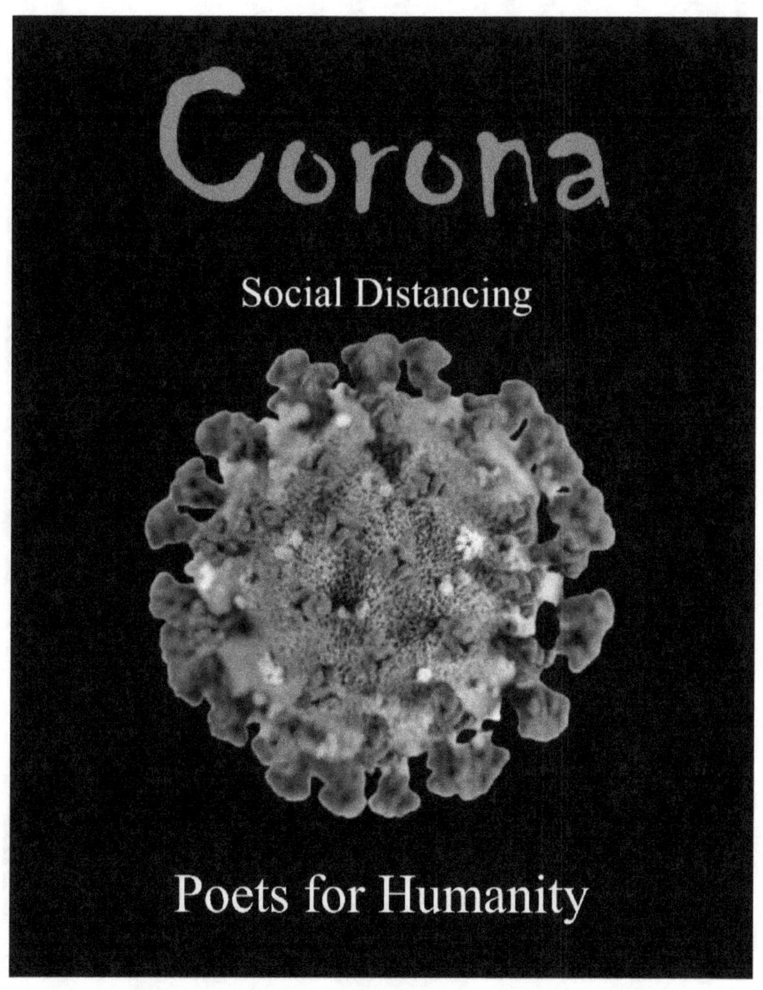
Corona
Social Distancing
Poets for Humanity

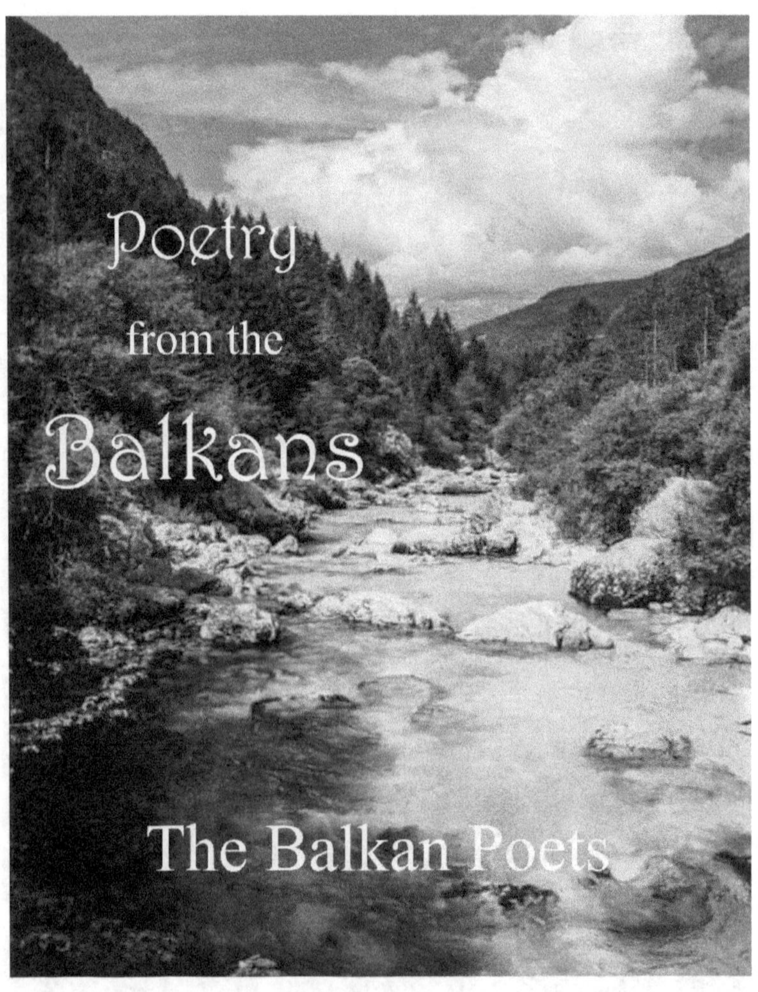
Poetry
from the
Balkans
The Balkan Poets

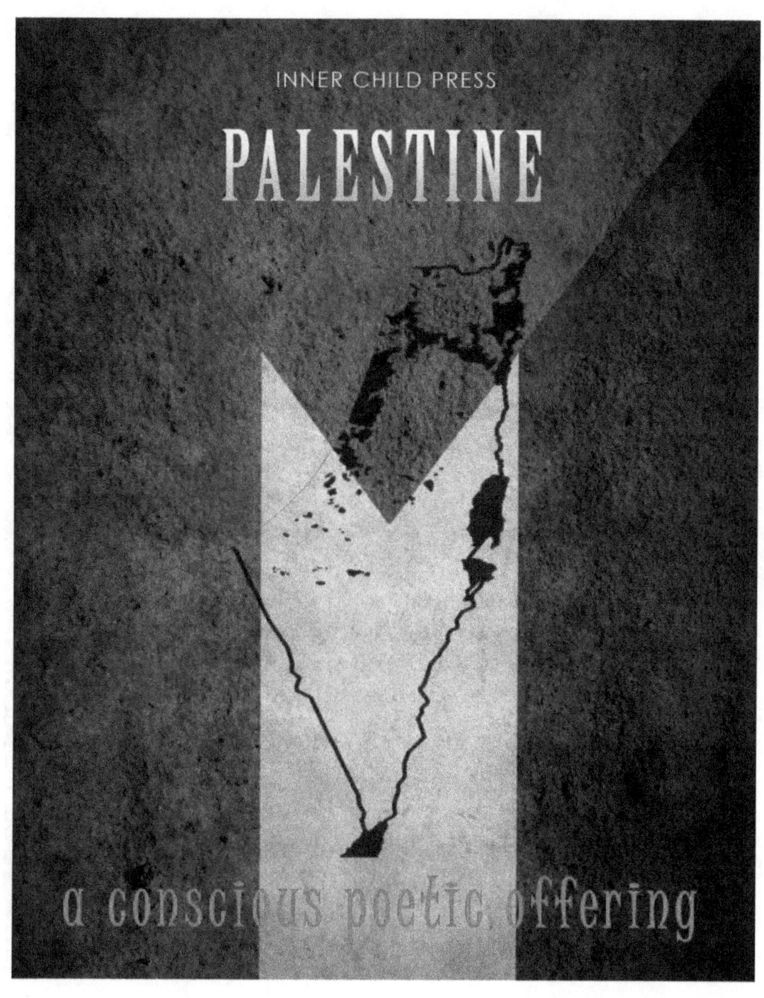
INNER CHILD PRESS
PALESTINE
a conscious poetic offering

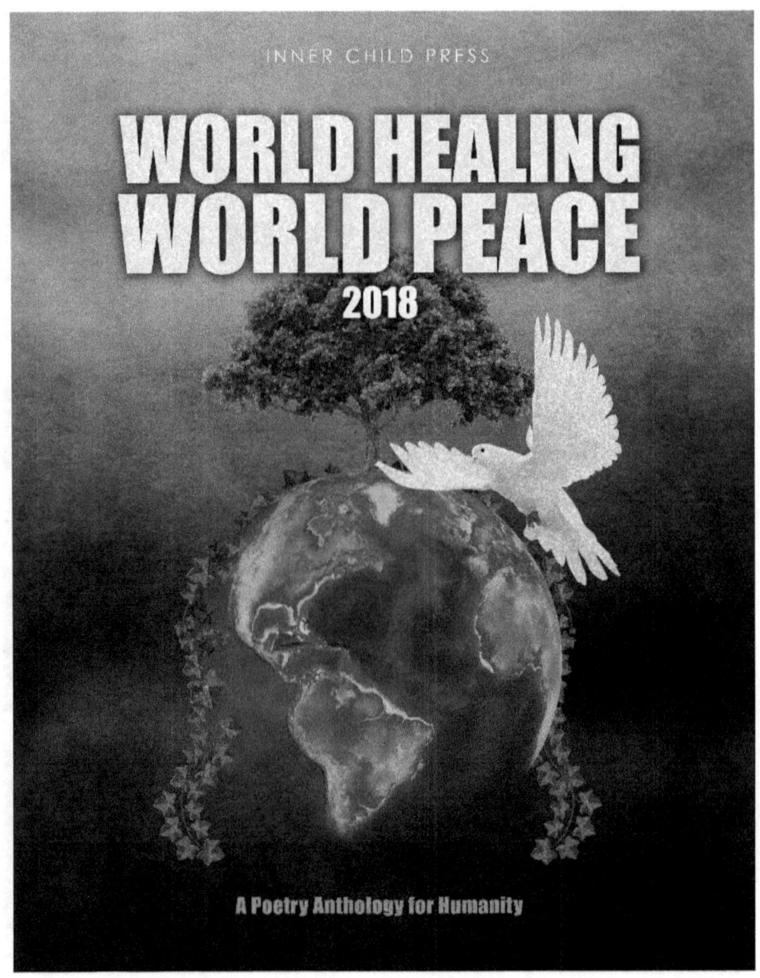
INNER CHILD PRESS
WORLD HEALING
WORLD PEACE
2018
A Poetry Anthology for Humanity

Now Available at

www.innerchildpress.com

Inner Child Press International
presents
A Love Anthology
2019
The Love Poets

INNER CHILD PRESS
WORLD HEALING
WORLD PEACE
2018
A Poetry Anthology for Humanity

Now Available

www.worldhealingworldpeacepoetry.com

INNER CHILD PRESS
World Healing
World Peace
A Poetry Anthology 2014
Volume 1
INNER CHILD PRESS
World Healing
World Peace
A Poetry Anthology 2014
Volume 2

World Healing
World Peace
2012
A POETRY ANTHOLOGY
Volume 1
World Healing
World Peace
2012
A POETRY ANTHOLOGY
Volume 2

Now Available

www.worldhealingworldpeacepoetry.com

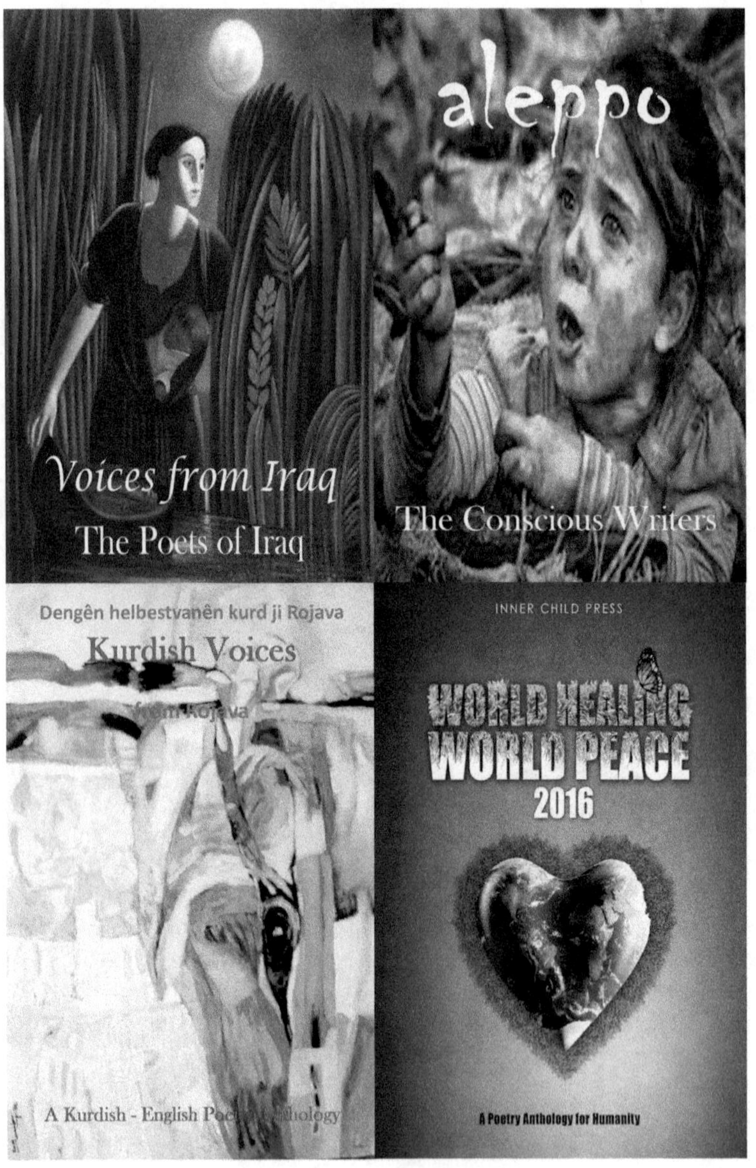
Voices from Iraq
The Poets of Iraq
aleppo
The Conscious Writers
Dengên helbestvanên kurd ji Rojava
Kurdish Voices
INNER CHILD PRESS
WORLD HEALING
WORLD PEACE
2016
A Poetry Anthology for Humanity

Now Available

www.innerchildpress.com/anthologies

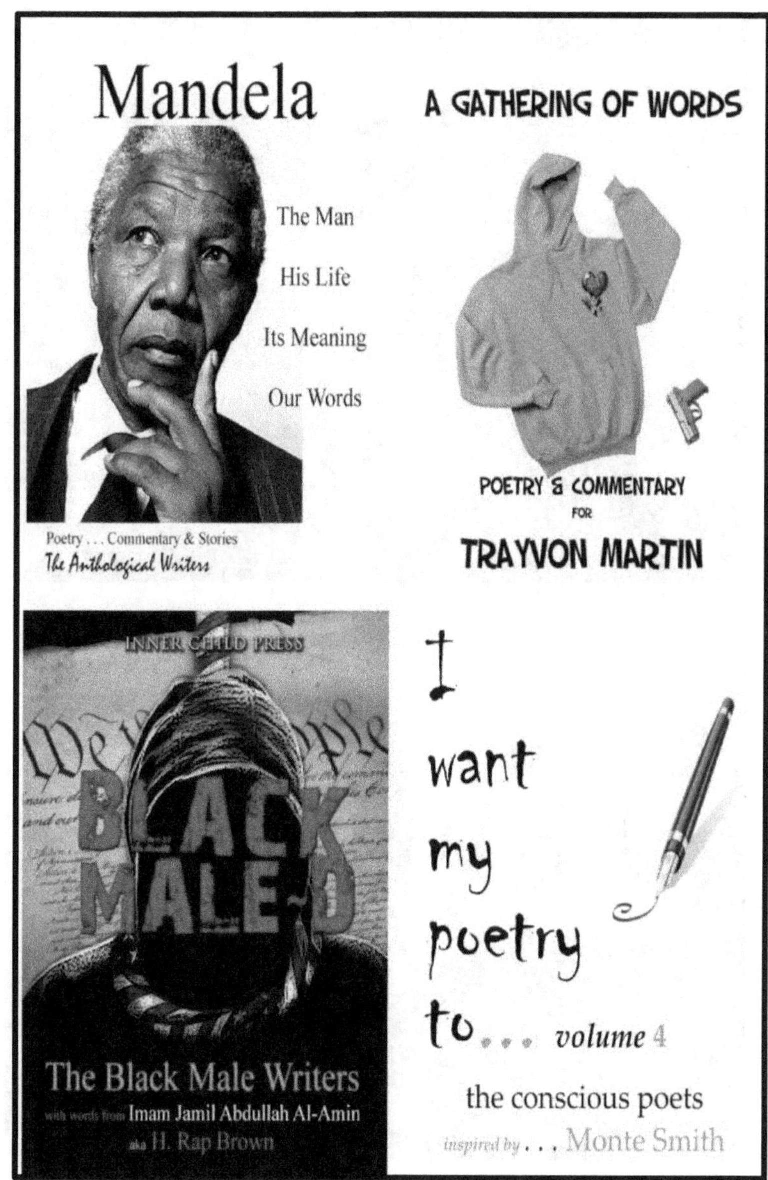
Mandela
The Man
His Life
Its Meaning
Our Words
Poetry . . . Commentary & Stories
The Anthological Writers
A GATHERING OF WORDS
POETRY & COMMENTARY
FOR
TRAYVON MARTIN
INNER CHILD PRESS
BLACK MALE-D
The Black Male Writers
Imam Jamil Abdullah Al-Amin
aka H. Rap Brown
I want my poetry to... volume 4
the conscious poets
inspired by . . . Monte Smith

Now Available

www.innerchildpress.com/anthologies

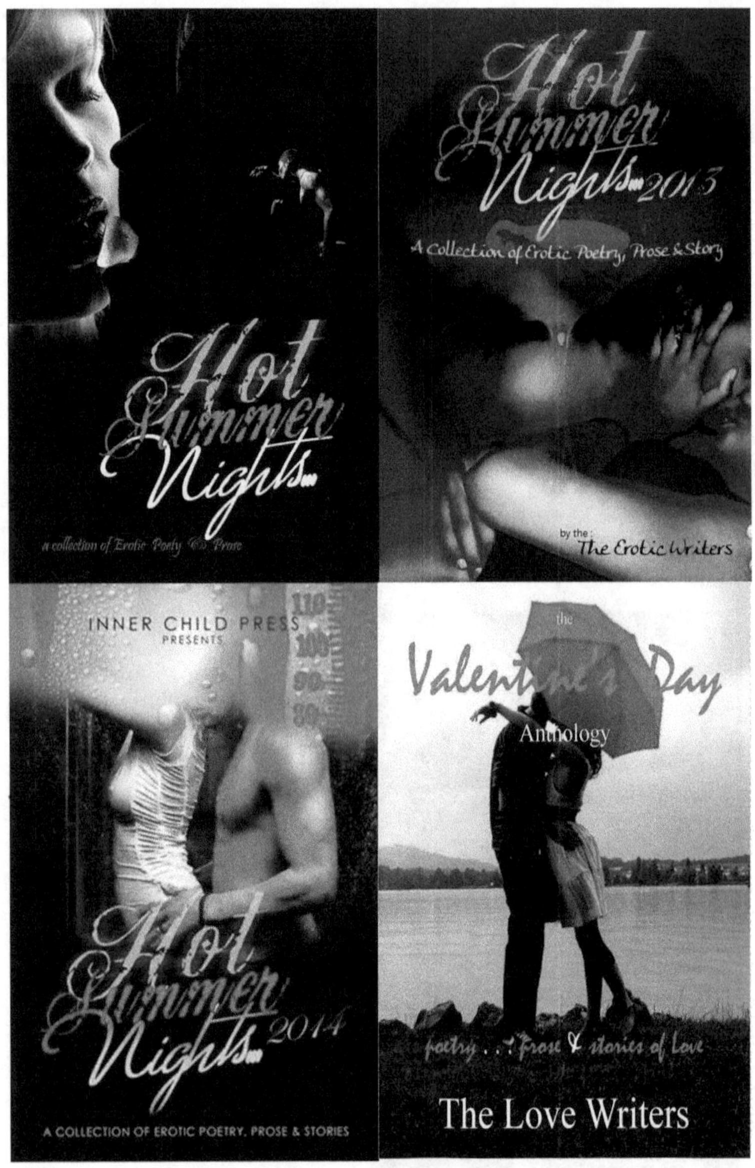
Hot Summer Nights...
a collection of Erotic Poetry & Prose
Hot Summer Nights... 2013
A Collection of Erotic Poetry, Prose & Story
by the :
The Erotic Writers
INNER CHILD PRESS
PRESENTS
Hot Summer Nights... 2014
A COLLECTION OF EROTIC POETRY, PROSE & STORIES
the
Valentine's Day
Anthology
poetry . . . prose & stories of Love
The Love Writers

Now Available

www.innerchildpress.com/anthologies

Janet
gone too soon . . .
healing through words
Poetry ... Prose ... Prayer ... Stories
a
Poetically
Spoken
Anthology
volume I
Collector's Edition
The Poetry Posse
Presents
an anthology
of
Love
The Poetry Posse 2016

Now Available

www.innerchildpress.com/anthologies

a collection of the Voices of Many inspired by . . .
Monte Smith
i want my
PoEtRy
to . . .
a collection of the Voices of Many inspired by . . .
Monte Smith
i want my
PoEtRy
to . . .
volume II
i want my
PoetRy
to . . . volume 3
a collection of the Voices of Many inspired by . . .
Monte Smith
11 Words
(9 lines . . .)
for those who are challenged
an anthology of Poetry inspired by . . .
Poetry Dancer

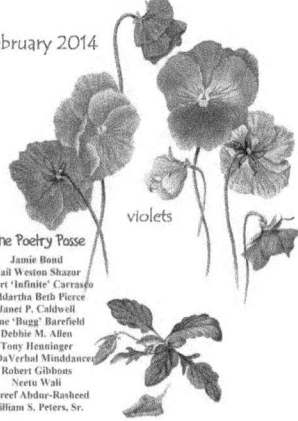

the year of the poet
May 2014
May's Featured Poets
ReeCee
Joski the Poet
Shannon Stanton
Dedicated To our Children
The Poetry Posse
Lily of the Valley

the Year of the Poet
June 2014
Love & Relationship
Rose
June's Featured Poets
Shantelle McLin
Jacqueline D. E. Kennedy
Abraham N. Benjamin
The Poetry Posse
Jamie Bond
Gail Weston Shazor
Albert 'Infinite' Carrasco
Siddartha Beth Pierce
Janet P. Caldwell
June 'Bugg' Barefield
Debbie M. Allen
Tony Henninger
Joe DaVerbal Minddancer
Robert Gibbons
Neetu Wali
Shareef Abdur-Rasheed
Kimberly Burnham
William S. Peters, Sr.

The Year of the Poet
July 2014
July Feature Poets
Christena A. V. Williams
Dr. John R. Strum
Kolade Olanrewaju Freedom
The Poetry Posse
Jamie Bond
Gail Weston Shazor
Siddartha Beth Pierce
Janet P. Caldwell
June 'Bugg' Barefield
Debbie M. Allen
Tony Henninger
Joe DaVerbal Minddancer
Robert Gibbons
Neetu Wali
Shareef Abdur-Rasheed
Kimberly Burnham
William S. Peters, Sr.
Lotus
Asian Flower of the Month

The Year of the Poet
August 2014
Gladiolus
The Poetry Posse
Jamie Bond
Gail Weston Shazor
Albert 'Infinite' Carrasco
Siddartha Beth Pierce
Janet P. Caldwell
June 'Bugg' Barefield
Debbie M. Allen
Tony Henninger
Joe DaVerbal Minddancer
Robert Gibbons
Neetu Wali
Shareef Abdur-Rasheed
Kimberly Burnham
William S. Peters, Sr.
August Feature Poets
Ann White * Rosalind Cherry * Sheila Jenkins

Now Available

www.innerchildpress.com/the-year-of-the-poet

The Year of the Poet
September 2014
Aster
Morning-Glory
September Feature Poets
Florence Malone * Keith Alan Hamilton
The Poetry Posse
Jamie Bond * Gail Weston Shazor * Albert 'Infinite' Carrasco * Siddartha Beth Pierce
Janet P. Caldwell * June 'Bugg' Barefield * Debbie M. Allen * Tony Henninger
Joe DaVerbal Minddancer * Robert Gibbons * Neetu Wali * Shareef Abdur-Rasheed
Kimberly Burnham * William S. Peters, Sr.

The Year of the Poet
October 2014
Red Poppy
The Poetry Posse
Jamie Bond * Gail Weston Shazor * Albert 'Infinite' Carrasco * Siddartha Beth Pierce
Janet P. Caldwell * June 'Bugg' Barefield * Debbie M. Allen * Tony Henninger
Joe DaVerbal Minddancer * Robert Gibbons * Neetu Wali * Shareef Abdur-Rasheed
Kimberly Burnham * William S. Peters, Sr.
October Feature Poets
Ceri Naz * Rajendra Padhi * Elizabeth Castillo

The Year of the Poet
November 2014
Chrysanthemum
The Poetry Posse
November Feature Poets
Jocelyn Mosman * Jackie Allen * James Moore * Neville Hiatt

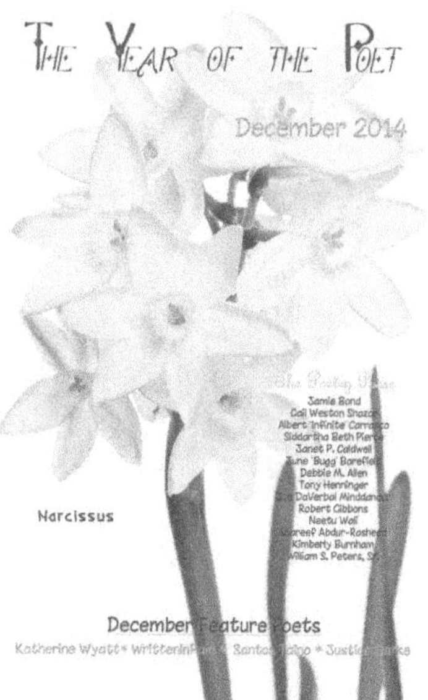
The Year of the Poet
December 2014
Narcissus

Now Available

www.innerchildpress.com/the-year-of-the-poet

The Year of the Poet II
January 2015
The Poetry Posse
Jamie Bond
Gail Weston Shazor
Albert 'Infinite' Carrasco
Siddartha Beth Pierce
Janet P. Caldwell
Tony Henninger
Garnet
Robert Gibbons
Neetu Wali
Shareef Abdur – Rasheed
Kimberly Burnham
Ann White
Keith Alan Hamilton
Katherine Wyatt
Fahredin Shehu
Hülya N. Yılmaz
Teresa E. Gallion
Jackie Allen
William S. Peters, Sr.
January Feature Poets
Bismay Mohanti * Jen Walls * Eric Judah

THE YEAR OF THE POET II

February 2015

Amethyst
THE POETRY POSSE
Jamie Bond
Gail Weston Shazor
Albert 'Infinite' Carrasco
Siddartha Beth Pierce
Janet P. Caldwell
Tony Henninger
Joe DaVerbal Minddancer
Robert Gibbons
Neetu Wali
Shareef Abdur – Rasheed
Kimberly Burnham
Ann White
Keith Alan Hamilton
Katherine Wyatt

FEBRUARY FEATURE POETS

Iram Fatima * Bob McNeil * Kerstin Centervall

The Year of the Poet II

March 2015

Our Featured Poets

Heung Sook * Anthony Arnold * Alicia Poland

Bloodstone

The Poetry Posse 2015

Jamie Bond * Gail Weston Shazor * Albert 'Infinite' Carrasco
Siddartha Beth Pierce * Janet P. Caldwell * Tony Henninger
Joe DaVerbal Minddancer * Neetu Wali * Shareef Abdur – Rasheed
Kimberly Burnham * Ann White * Keith Alan Hamilton
Katherine Wyatt * Fahredin Shehu * Hülya N. Yılmaz
Teresa E. Gallion * Jackie Allen * William S. Peters, Sr.

The Year of the Poet II
April 2015
Celebrating International Poetry Month
Our Featured Poets
Raja Williams * Dennis Ferado * Laure Charazac
Diamonds
The Poetry Posse 2015
Jamie Bond * Gail Weston Shazor * Albert 'Infinite' Carrasco
Siddartha Beth Pierce * Janet P. Caldwell * Tony Henninger
Joe DaVerbal Minddancer * Neetu Wali * Shareef Abdur – Rasheed
Kimberly Burnham * Ann White * Keith Alan Hamilton
Katherine Wyatt * Fahredin Shehu * Hülya N. Yılmaz
Teresa E. Gallion * Jackie Allen * William S. Peters, Sr.

Now Available

www.innerchildpress.com/the-year-of-the-poet

The Year of the Poet II
May 2015
May's Featured Poets
Geri Algeri
Akin Mosi Chinnery
Anna Jakubczak
Emeralds
The Poetry Posse 2015
Jamie Bond * Gail Weston Shazor * Albert 'Infinite' Carrasco
Siddartha Beth Pierce * Janet P. Caldwell * Tony Henninger
Joe DaVerbal Minddancer * Neetu Wali * Shareef Abdur – Rasheed
Kimberly Burnham * Ann White * Keith Alan Hamilton
Katherine Wyatt * Fahredin Shehu * Hülya N. Yılmaz
Teresa E. Gallion * Jackie Allen * William S. Peters, Sr.

The Year of the Poet II

June 2015

June's Featured Poets

Anahit Arustamyan * Yvette D. Murrell * Regina A. Walker

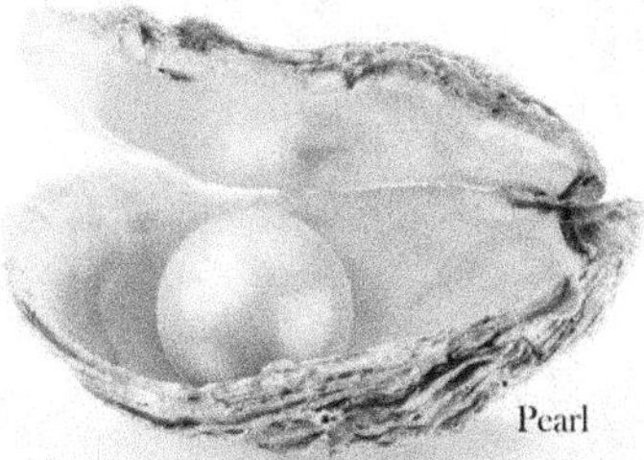

Pearl

The Poetry Posse 2015

Jamie Bond * Gail Weston Shazor * Albert 'Infinite' Carrasco
Siddartha Beth Pierce * Janet P. Caldwell * Tony Henninger
Joe DaVerbal Minddancer * Neetu Wali * Shareef Abdur – Rasheed
Kimberly Burnham * Ann White * Keith Alan Hamilton
Katherine Wyatt * Fahredin Shehu * Hülya N. Yılmaz
Teresa E. Gallion * Jackie Allen * William S. Peters, Sr.

The Year of the Poet II

July 2015

The Featured Poets for July 2015

Abhik Shome * Christina Neal * Robert Neal

Rubies

The Poetry Posse 2015

Jamie Bond * Gail Weston Shazor * Albert 'Infinite' Carrasco
Siddartha Beth Pierce * Janet P. Caldwell * Tony Henninger
Joe DaVerbal Minddancer * Neetu Wali * Shareef Abdur – Rasheed
Kimberly Burnham * Ann White * Keith Alan Hamilton
Katherine Wyatt * Fahredin Shehu * Hülya N. Yılmaz
Teresa E. Gallion * Jackie Allen * William S. Peters, Sr.

The Year of the Poet II

August 2015

Peridot

Featured Poets
Gayle Howell
Ann Chalasz
Christopher Schultz

The Poetry Posse 2015

Jamie Bond * Gail Weston Shazor * Albert 'Infinite' Carrasco
Siddartha Beth Pierce * Janet P. Caldwell * Tony Henninger
Joe DaVerbal Minddancer * Neetu Wali * Shareef Abdur – Rasheed
Kimberly Burnham * Ann White * Keith Alan Hamilton
Katherine Wyatt * Fahredin Shehu * Hülya N. Yılmaz
Teresa E. Gallion * Jackie Allen * William S. Peters, Sr.

Now Available

www.innerchildpress.com/the-year-of-the-poet

The Year of the Poet II
September 2015
Featured Poets
Alfreda Ghee * Lonneice Weeks Badley * Demetrios Trifiatis
Sapphires
The Poetry Posse 2015
Jamie Bond * Gail Weston Shazor * Albert 'Infinite' Carrasco
Siddartha Beth Pierce * Janet P. Caldwell * Tony Henninger
Joe DaVerbal Minddancer * Neetu Wali * Shareef Abdur – Rasheed
Kimberly Burnham * Ann White * Keith Alan Hamilton
Katherine Wyatt * Fahredin Shehu * Hülya N. Yılmaz
Teresa E. Gallion * Jackie Allen * William S. Peters, Sr.
The Year of the Poet II
October 2015
Featured Poets
Monte Smith * Laura J. Wolfe * William Washington
Opal
The Poetry Posse 2015
Jamie Bond * Gail Weston Shazor * Albert 'Infinite' Carrasco
Siddartha Beth Pierce * Janet P. Caldwell * Tony Henninger
Joe DaVerbal Minddancer * Neetu Wali * Shareef Abdur – Rasheed
Kimberly Burnham * Ann White * Keith Alan Hamilton
Katherine Wyatt * Fahredin Shehu * Hülya N. Yılmaz
Teresa E. Gallion * Jackie Allen * William S. Peters, Sr.

The Year of the Poet II
November 2015
Featured Poets
Alan W. Jankowski
Bismay Mohanty
James Moore
Topaz
The Poetry Posse 2015
Jamie Bond * Gail Weston Shazor * Albert 'Infinite' Carrasco
Siddartha Beth Pierce * Janet P. Caldwell * Tony Henninger
Joe DaVerbal Minddancer * Neetu Wali * Shareef Abdur – Rasheed
Kimberly Burnham * Ann White * Keith Alan Hamilton
Katherine Wyatt * Fahredin Shehu * Hülya N. Yılmaz
Teresa E. Gallion * Jackie Allen * William S. Peters, Sr.

The Year of the Poet II
December 2015

Featured Poets
Kerione Bryan * Michelle Joan Barulich * Neville Hiatt

Turquoise

The Poetry Posse 2015
Jamie Bond * Gail Weston Shazor * Albert 'Infinite' Carrasco
Siddartha Beth Pierce * Janet P. Caldwell * Tony Henninger
Joe DaVerbal Minddancer * Neetu Wali * Shareef Abdur – Rasheed
Kimberly Burnham * Ann White * Keith Alan Hamilton
Katherine Wyatt * Fahredin Shehu * Hülya N. Yılmaz
Teresa E. Gallion * Jackie Allen * William S. Peters, Sr.

Now Available

www.innerchildpress.com/the-year-of-the-poet

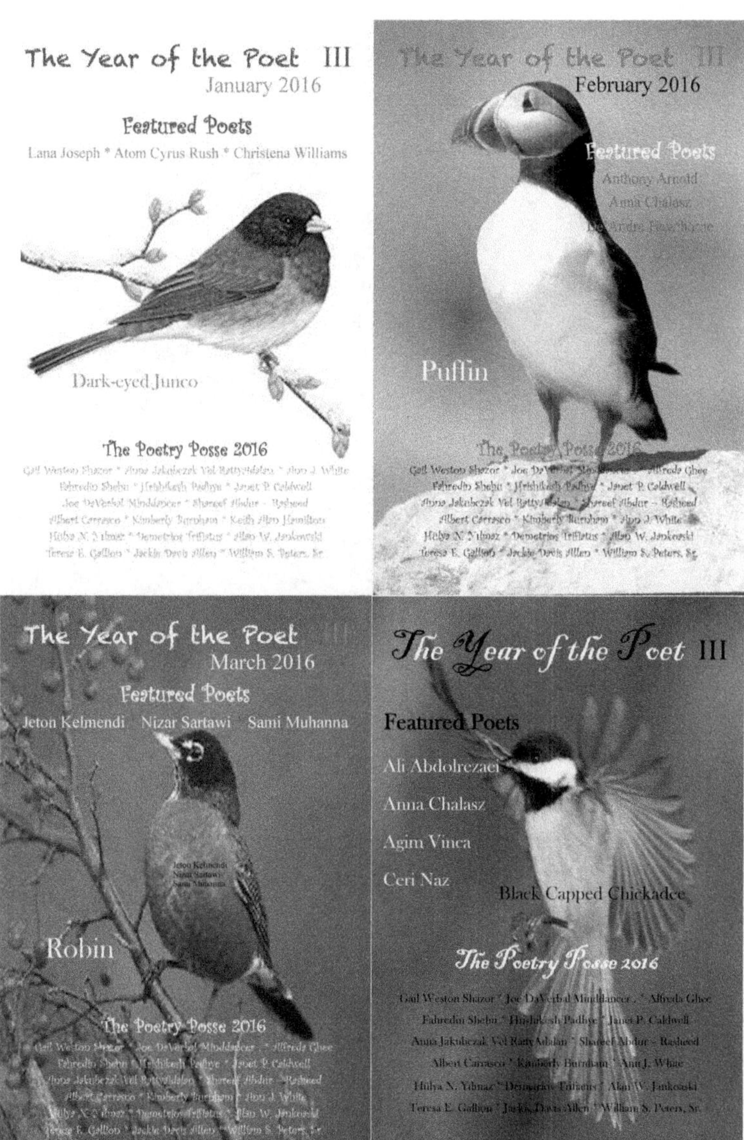
The Year of the Poet III
January 2016
Featured Poets
Lana Joseph * Atom Cyrus Rush * Christena Williams
Dark-eyed Junco
The Poetry Posse 2016
The Year of the Poet III
February 2016
Featured Poets
Anthony Arnold
Anna Chalasz
Puffin
The Year of the Poet
March 2016
Featured Poets
Jeton Kelmendi Nizar Sartawi Sami Muhanna
Robin
The Poetry Posse 2016
The Year of the Poet III
Featured Poets
Ali Abdolrezaei
Anna Chalasz
Agim Vinca
Ceri Naz
Black Capped Chickadee
The Poetry Posse 2016
celebrating international poetry month

Now Available

www.innerchildpress.com/the-year-of-the-poet

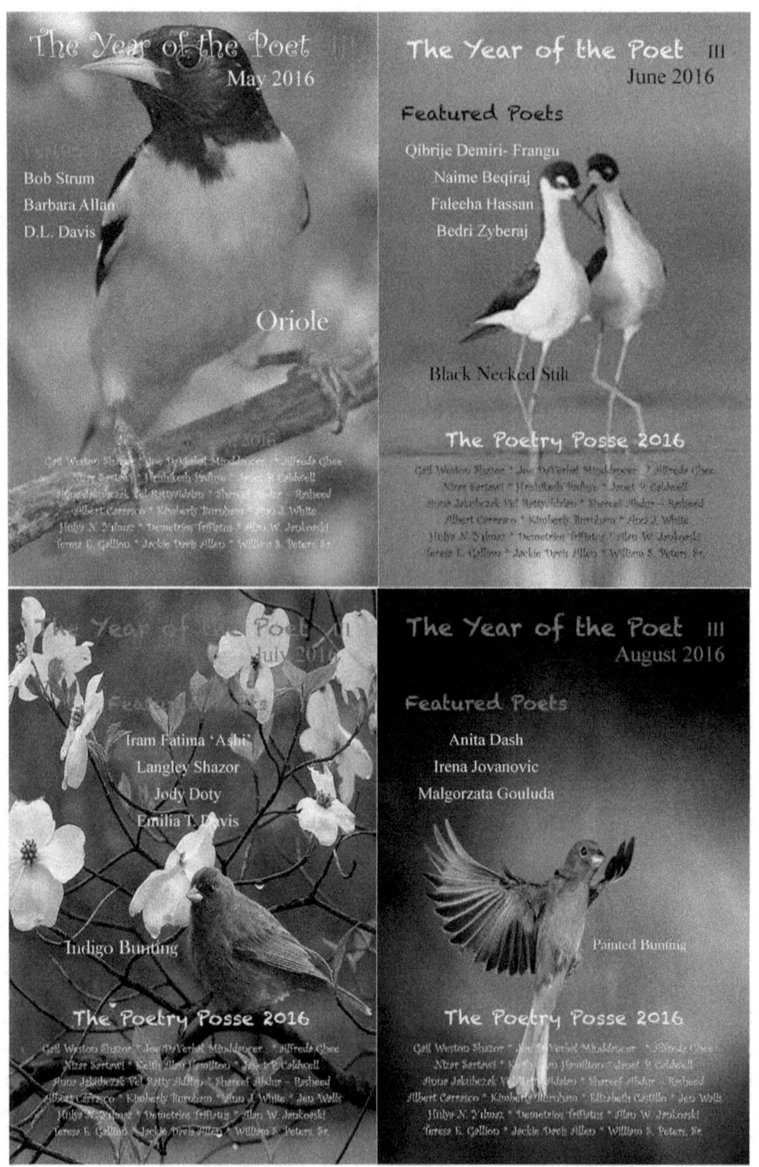
The Year of the Poet
May 2016
Bob Strum
Barbara Allan
D.L. Davis
Oriole
The Year of the Poet III
June 2016
Featured Poets
Qibrije Demiri- Frangu
Naime Beqiraj
Faleeha Hassan
Bedri Zyberaj
Black Necked Stilt
The Poetry Posse 2016
Iram Fatima 'Ashi'
Langley Shazor
Jody Doty
Indigo Bunting
The Poetry Posse 2016
The Year of the Poet III
August 2016
Featured Poets
Anita Dash
Irena Jovanovic
Malgorzata Gouluda
Painted Bunting
The Poetry Posse 2016

Now Available

www.innerchildpress.com/the-year-of-the-poet

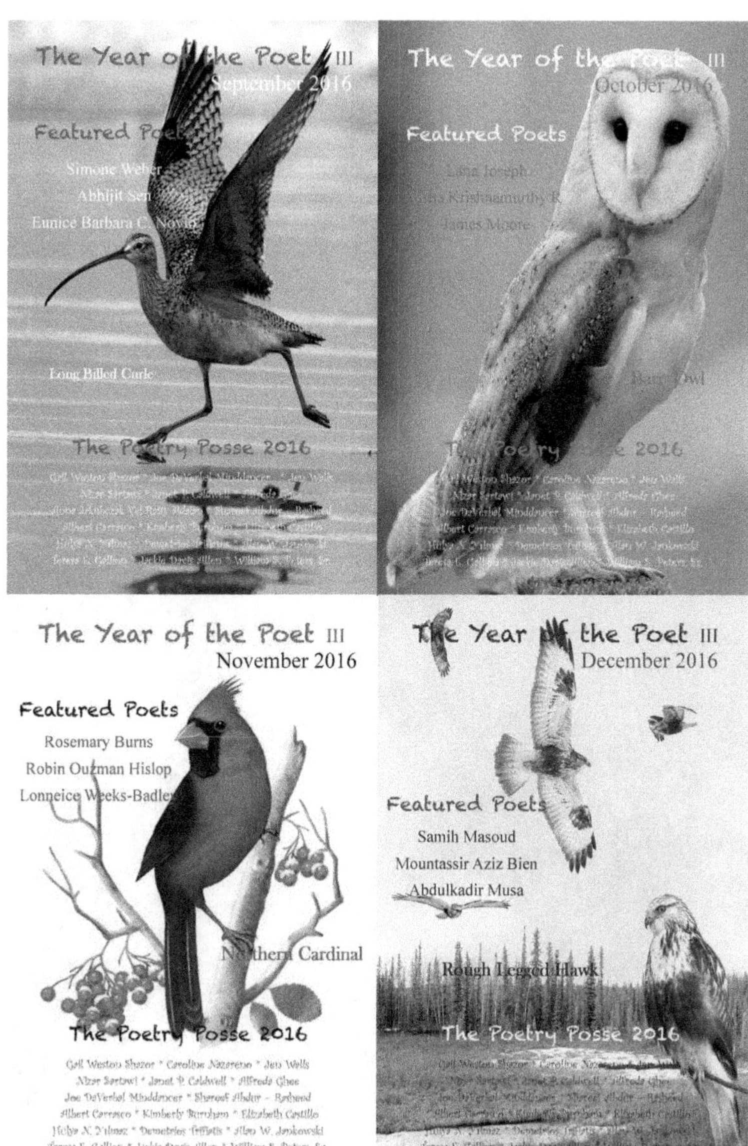
The Year of the Poet III
September 2016
Featured Poets
Simone Weber
Abhijit Sen
Eunice Barbara C. Novio
The Poetry Posse 2016
The Year of the Poet III
October 2016
Featured Poets
The Poetry Posse 2016
The Year of the Poet III
November 2016
Featured Poets
Rosemary Burns
Robin Ouzman Hislop
Lonneice Weeks-Badley
Northern Cardinal
The Poetry Posse 2016
The Year of the Poet III
December 2016
Featured Poets
Samih Masoud
Mountassir Aziz Bien
Abdulkadir Musa
Rough Legged Hawk
The Poetry Posse 2016

Now Available

www.innerchildpress.com/the-year-of-the-poet

Inner Child Press Anthologies

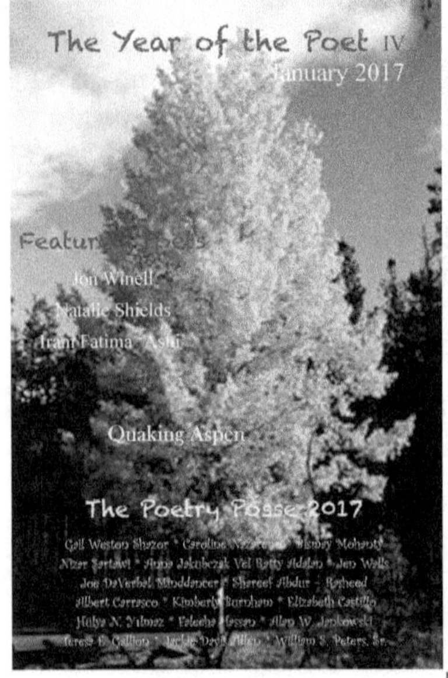

The Year of the Poet IV
January 2017
Featured Poets
Jon Winell
Natalie Shields
Iram Fatima "Ashi"
Quaking Aspen
The Poetry Posse 2017

The Year of the Poet IV
February 2017
Featured Poets
Lin Ross
Soukaina Fathi
Anwer Ghani
Witch Hazel
The Poetry Posse 2017
Gail Weston Shazor * Caroline Nazareno * Bismay Mohanty
Nizar Sartawi * Anna Jakubczak Vel Ratty Adalan * Jen Walls
Joe DaVerbal Minddancer * Shareef Abdur – Rasheed
Albert Carrasco * Kimberly Burnham * Elizabeth Castillo
Hulya N. Yilmaz * Faleeha Hassan * Alan W. Jankowski
Teresa E. Gallion * Jackie Davis Allen * William S. Peters, Sr.

The Year of the Poet IV
March 2017
Featured Poets
Tremell Stevens
Francisca Ricinski
Jamil Abu Shaih
The Eastern Redbud
The Poetry Posse 2017
Gail Weston Shazor * Caroline Nazareno * Bismay Mohanty
Teresa E. Gallion * Anna Jakubczak Vel Ratty Adalan
Joe DaVerbal Minddancer * Shareef Abdur – Rasheed
Albert Carrasco * Kimberly Burnham * Elizabeth Castillo
Hulya N. Yilmaz * Faleeha Hassan * Jackie Davis Allen
Jen Walls * Nizar Sartawi * * William S. Peters, Sr.

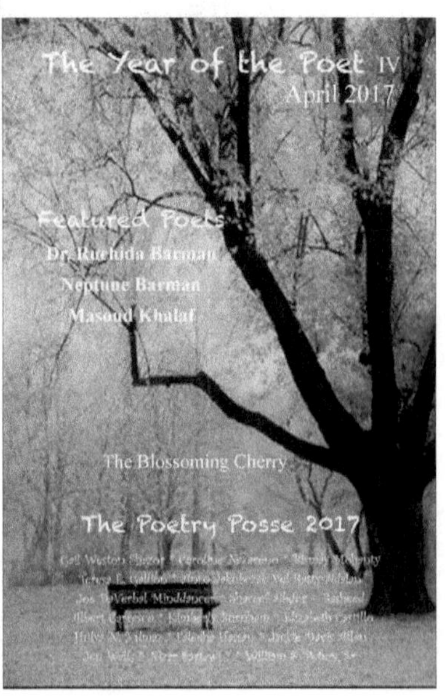

The Year of the Poet IV
April 2017
Featured Poets
Dr. Ruchida Barman
Neptune Barman
Masoud Khalaf
The Blossoming Cherry
The Poetry Posse 2017

Now Available

www.innerchildpress.com/the-year-of-the-poet

Inner Child Press Anthologies

The Year of the Poet IV
May 2017
The Flowering Dogwood Tree
Featured Poets
Kallisa Powell
Alicja Maria Kuberska
Fethi Sassi
The Poetry Posse 2017

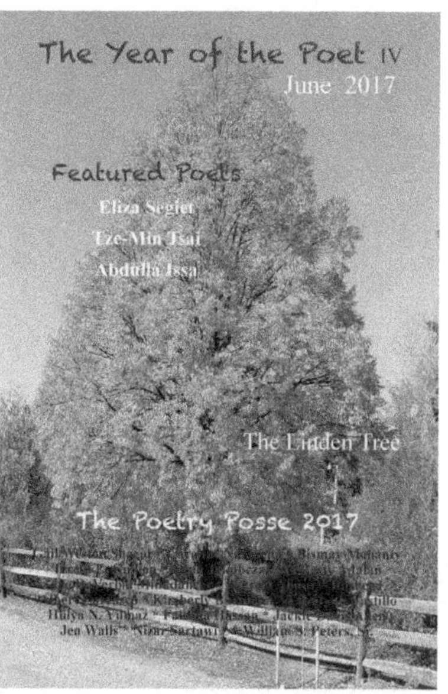

The Year of the Poet IV
June 2017
Featured Poets
Eliza Segiet
Tze-Min Tsai
Abdulla Issa
The Linden Tree
The Poetry Posse 2017

The Year of the Poet IV
July 2017
Featured Poets
Anca Mihaela Bruma
Ibaa Ismail
Zvonko Taneski
The Oak Moon
The Poetry Posse 2017

The Year of the Poet IV
August 2017
Jonathan Aquino
Kitty Hsu
Langley Shazor
The Hazelnut Tree
The Poetry Posse 2017

Now Available

www.innerchildpress.com/the-year-of-the-poet

The Year of the Poet IV

September 2017

Featured Poets

Martina Reisz Newber

Ameer Nassir

Christine Fulco Neal

Robert Neal

The Elm Tree

The Poetry Posse 2017

Gail Weston Shazor * Caroline Nazareno * Bismay Mohanty
Teresa E. Gallion * Anna Jakubczak Vel Ratty Adalan
Joe DaVerbal Minddancer * Shareef Abdur – Rasheed
Albert Carrasco * Kimberly Burnham * Elizabeth Castillo
Hülya N. Yılmaz * Faleeha Hassan * Jackie Davis Allen
Jen Walls * Nizar Sartawi * * William S. Peters, Sr.

The Year of the Poet IV

October 2017

Featured Poets

Ahmed Abu Saleem

Nedal Al-Qaeim

Sadeddin Sh

The Black Walnut Tree

The Poetry Posse 2017

Gail Weston Shazor * Caroline Nazareno * Bismay Mohanty
Teresa E. Gallion * Anna Jakubczak Vel Ratty Adalan
Joe DaVerbal Minddancer * Shareef Abdur – Rasheed
Albert Carrasco * Kimberly Burnham * Elizabeth Castillo
Hülya N. Yılmaz * Faleeha Hassan * Jackie Davis Allen
Jen Walls * Nizar Sartawi * * William S. Peters, Sr.

The Year of the Poet IV

November 2017

Featured Poets

Kay Peters

Alfreda D. Ghee

Gabriella Garofalo

Rosemary Cappello

The Tree of Life

The Poetry Posse 2017

Gail Weston Shazor * Caroline Nazareno * Bismay Mohanty
Teresa E. Gallion * Anna Jakubczak Vel Ratty Adalan
Joe DaVerbal Minddancer * Shareef Abdur – Rasheed
Albert Carrasco * Kimberly Burnham * Elizabeth Castillo
Hülya N. Yılmaz * Faleeha Hassan * Jackie Davis Allen
Jen Walls * Nizar Sartawi * William S. Peters, Sr.

The Year of the Poet IV

December 2017

Featured Poets

Justice Clarke

Mariel M. Pabroa

Kiley Brown

The Fig Tree

The Poetry Posse 2017

Gail Weston Shazor * Caroline Nazareno * Bismay Mohanty
Teresa E. Gallion * Anna Jakubczak Vel Ratty Adalan
Joe DaVerbal Minddancer * Shareef Abdur – Rasheed
Albert Carrasco * Kimberly Burnham * Elizabeth Castillo
Hülya N. Yılmaz * Faleeha Hassan * Jackie Davis Allen
Jen Walls * Nizar Sartawi * William S. Peters, Sr.

Now Available

www.innerchildpress.com/the-year-of-the-poet

The Year of the Poet V
January 2018
Featured Poets
Iyad Shamasnah
Yasmeen Hamzeh
Ali Abdolrezaei
Aksum
The Poetry Posse 2018
The Year of the Poet V
February 2018
Sabean
Featured Poets
Muhammad Azram
Anna Szawracka
Abhilipsa Kuanar
Aanika Aery
The Poetry Posse 2018
Gail Weston Shazor * Caroline Nazareno * Tezmin Ition Tsai
Hülya N. Yılmaz * Faleeha Hassan * Jackie Davis Allen
Teresa E. Gallion * Anna Jakubczak Vel Ratty Adalan
Alicja Maria Kuberska * Shareef Abdur – Rasheed
Kimberly Burnham * Elizabeth Castillo
Nizar Sartawi * William S. Peters, Sr.
The Year of the Poet V
March 2018
Featured Poets
Iram Fatima 'Ashi'
Cassandra Swan
Jaleel Khazaal
Shazia Zaman
Mexico
Cuba
Belize
Jamaica
Haiti
Puerto Rico
Nicaragua
Panama
Costa Rica
Caribbean
&
Middle America
The Poetry Posse 2018
Gail Weston Shazor * Nizar Sartawi * Hülya N. Yılmaz
Jackie Davis Allen * Caroline 'Ceri' Nazareno
Alicja Maria Kuberska * Teresa E. Gallion
Faleeha Hassan * Shareef Abdur – Rasheed
Kimberly Burnham * Elizabeth Castillo
Tezmin Ition Tsai * William S. Peters, Sr.
The Year of the Poet V
April 2018
Featured Poets
The Nez Perce

Now Available

www.innerchildpress.com/the-year-of-the-poet

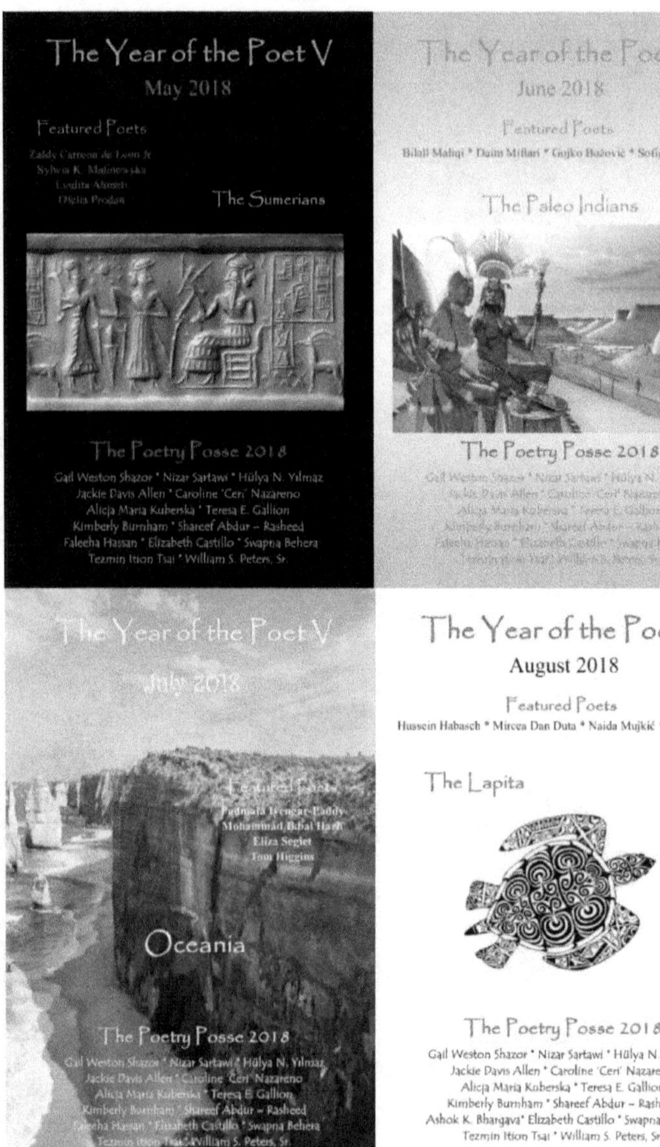
The Year of the Poet V
May 2018
Featured Poets
The Sumerians
The Poetry Posse 2018
Gail Weston Shazor * Nizar Sartawi * Hülya N. Yılmaz
Jackie Davis Allen * Caroline 'Ceri' Nazareno
Alicja Maria Kuberska * Teresa E. Gallion
Kimberly Burnham * Shareef Abdur – Rasheed
Faleeha Hassan * Elizabeth Castillo * Swapna Behera
Tezmin Ition Tsai * William S. Peters, Sr.
The Year of the Poet V
June 2018
Featured Poets
The Paleo Indians
The Poetry Posse 2018
The Year of the Poet V
July 2018
Oceania
The Poetry Posse 2018
The Year of the Poet V
August 2018
Featured Poets
Hussein Habasch * Mircea Dan Duta * Naida Mujkić * Swagat Das
The Lapita
The Poetry Posse 2018
Gail Weston Shazor * Nizar Sartawi * Hülya N. Yılmaz
Jackie Davis Allen * Caroline 'Ceri' Nazareno
Alicja Maria Kuberska * Teresa E. Gallion
Kimberly Burnham * Shareef Abdur – Rasheed
Ashok K. Bhargava* Elizabeth Castillo * Swapna Behaera
Tezmin Ition Tsai * William S. Peters, Sr.

Now Available

www.innerchildpress.com/the-year-of-the-poet

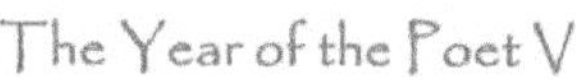
The Year of the Poet V

September 2018

The Aztecs & Incas

Featured Poets

The Poetry Posse 2018

Gail Weston Shazor * Nizar Sartawi * Hülya N. Yılmaz
Jackie Davis Allen * Caroline 'Ceri' Nazareno
Alicja Maria Kuberska * Teresa E. Gallion
Kimberly Burnham * Shareef Abdur – Rasheed
Ashok K. Bhargava * Elizabeth Castillo * Swapna Behaera
Tezmin Ition Tsai * William S. Peters, Sr.

The Year of the Poet V
October 2018
Featured Poets
Alicia Minjarez * Lonneice Weeks-Badley
Lopamudra Mishra * Abdelwahed Souayah
Bengali
The Poetry Posse 2018
Gail Weston Shazor * Nizar Sartawi * Hülya N. Yılmaz
Jackie Davis Allen * Caroline 'Ceri' Nazareno
Alicja Maria Kuberska * Teresa E. Gallion
Kimberly Burnham * Shareef Abdur – Rasheed
Ashok K. Bhargava * Elizabeth Castillo * Swapna Behaera
Tezmin Ition Tsai * William S. Peters, Sr.

The Year of the Poet V
November 2018
Featured Poets
Michelle Joan Barulich * Monsif Beroual
Krystyna Konecka * Nassira Nezzar
The Poetry Posse 2018

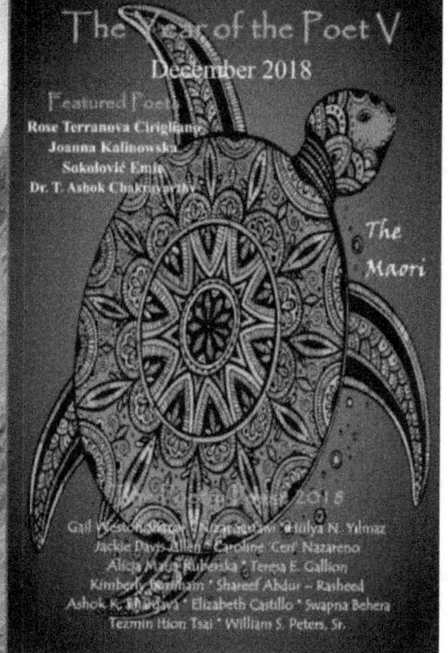
December 2018
Joanna Kalinowska
The Maori
Jackie Davis Allen * Caroline 'Ceri' Nazareno
Kimberly Burnham * Shareef Abdur – Rasheed
Tezmin Ition Tsai * William S. Peters, Sr.

Now Available

www.innerchildpress.com/the-year-of-the-poet

Inner Child Press Anthologies

The Year of the Poet VI

January 2019

Indigenous North Americans

Featured Poets

Houda Elfchtali
Anthony Briscoe
Iram Fatima 'Ashi'
Dr. K. K. Mathew

Dream Catcher

The Poetry Posse 2019

Gail Weston Shazor * Joe Paire * Hülya N. Yılmaz
Jackie Davis Allen * Caroline 'Ceri' Nazareno
Alicja Maria Kuberska * Teresa E. Gallion
Kimberly Burnham * Shareef Abdur – Rasheed
Ashok K. Bhargava * Elizabeth Castillo * Swapna Behera
Tezmin Ition Tsai * William S. Peters, Sr.

The Year of the Poet VI

February 2019

Featured Poets

Marek Lukaszewicz * Bharati Nayak
Aida G. Roque * Jean-Jacques Fournier

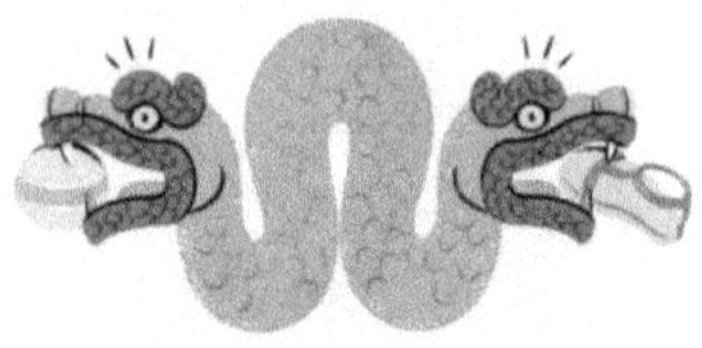

Meso-America

The Poetry Posse 2019

Gail Weston Shazor * Albert Carassco * Hülya N. Yılmaz
Jackie Davis Allen * Caroline Nazareno * Eliza Segiet
Alicja Maria Kuberska * Teresa E. Gallion * Joe Paire
Kimberly Burnham * Shareef Abdur – Rasheed
Ashok K. Bhargava * Elizabeth Castillo * Swapna Behera
Tezmin Ition Tsai * William S. Peters, Sr.

The Year of the Poet VI
March 2019
Featured Poets
Enesa Mahmić * Sylwia K. Malinowska
Shurouk Hammoud * Anwer Ghani
The Caribbean
The Poetry Posse 2019

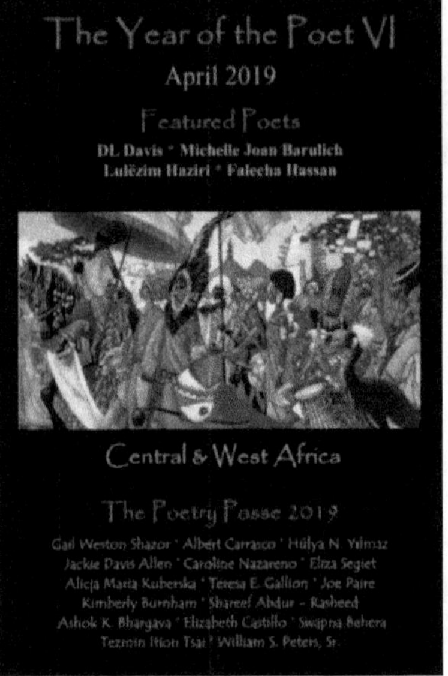
The Year of the Poet VI
April 2019
Featured Poets
DL Davis * Michelle Joan Barulich
Lulëzim Haziri * Falecha Hassan
Central & West Africa
The Poetry Posse 2019
Gail Weston Shazor * Albert Carrasco * Hülya N. Yılmaz
Jackie Davis Allen * Caroline Nazareno * Eliza Segiet
Alicja Maria Kuberska * Teresa E. Gallion * Joe Paire
Kimberly Burnham * Shareef Abdur – Rasheed
Ashok K. Bhargava * Elizabeth Castillo * Swapna Behera
Tezmin Ition Tsai * William S. Peters, Sr.

Now Available

www.innerchildpress.com/the-year-of-the-poet

The Year of the Poet VI
May 2019
Featured Poets
Emad Al-Haydary * Hussein Nasser Jabr
Wahab Sheriff * Abdul Razzaq Al Ameeri
Asia Southeast Asia and Maritime Asia
The Poetry Posse 2019
The Year of the Poet VI
June 2019
Featured Poets
Kate Gaudi Powiekszone * Sahaj Sabharwal
Iwu Jeff * Mohamed Abdel Aziz Shmeis
Arctic
Circumpolar
The Poetry Posse 2019
Gail Weston Shazor * Albert Carrasco * Hülya N. Yılmaz
Jackie Davis Allen * Caroline Nazareno * Eliza Segiet
Alicja Maria Kuberska * Teresa E. Gallion * Joe Paire
Kimberly Burnham * Shareef Abdur – Rasheed
Ashok K. Bhargava * Elizabeth Castillo * Swapna Behera
Tezmin Ition Tsai * William S. Peters, Sr.
The Year of the Poet VI
Featured Poets
The Horn of Africa
Ethiopia
Djibouti
Somalia
Eritrea
The Poetry Posse 2019
Gail Weston Shazor * Albert Carrasco * Hülya N. Yılmaz
Jackie Davis Allen * Caroline Nazareno * Eliza Segiet
Alicja Maria Kuberska * Teresa E. Gallion * Joe Paire
Kimberly Burnham * Shareef Abdur – Rasheed
Ashok K. Bhargava * Elizabeth Castillo * Swapna Behera
Tezmin Ition Tsai * William S. Peters, Sr.
The Year of the Poet VI
August 2019
Featured Poets
Shola Balogun * Bharati Nayak
Monalisa Dash Dwibedy * Mbizo Chirasha
Coexist
Southwest Asia
The Poetry Posse 2019
Gail Weston Shazor * Albert Carrasco * Hülya N. Yılmaz
Jackie Davis Allen * Caroline Nazareno * Eliza Segiet
Alicja Maria Kuberska * Teresa E. Gallion * Joe Paire
Kimberly Burnham * Shareef Abdur – Rasheed
Ashok K. Bhargava * Elizabeth Castillo * Swapna Behera
Tezmin Ition Tsai * William S. Peters, Sr.

Now Available

www.innerchildpress.com/the-year-of-the-poet

The Year of the Poet VI
September 2019
Featured Poets
Elena Liliana Popescu * Gobinda Biswas
Iram Fatima 'Ashi' * Joseph S. Spence, Sr.
The Caucasus
The Poetry Posse 2019
Gail Weston Shazor * Albert Carrasco * Hülya N. Yilmaz
Jackie Davis Allen * Caroline Nazareno * Eliza Segiet
Alicja Maria Kuberska * Teresa E. Gallion * Joe Paire
Kimberly Burnham * Shareef Abdur – Rasheed
Ashok K. Bhargava * Elizabeth Castillo * Swapna Behera
Tzemin Ition Tsai * William S. Peters, Sr.

The Year of the Poet VI
October 2019
Featured Poets
Ngozi Olivia Osuoha * Denisa Kondic
Pankhuri Sinha * Christena AV Williams
The Nile Valley
The Poetry Posse 2019

The Year of the Poet VI
November 2019
Featured Poets
Rozalia Aleksandrova * Orbindu Ganga
Smruti Ranjan Mohanty * Sofia Skleida
China
East Asia
Northern Asia
The Poetry Posse 2019

The Year of the Poet VI
December 2019
Featured Poets
Oceania
The Poetry Posse 2019
Gail Weston Shazor * Albert Carrasco * Hülya N. Yilmaz
Jackie Davis Allen * Caroline Nazareno * Eliza Segiet
Alicja Maria Kuberska * Teresa E. Gallion * Joe Paire
Kimberly Burnham * Shareef Abdur – Rasheed
Ashok K. Bhargava * Elizabeth Castillo * Swapna Behera
Tzemin Ition Tsai * William S. Peters, Sr.

Now Available

www.innerchildpress.com/the-year-of-the-poet

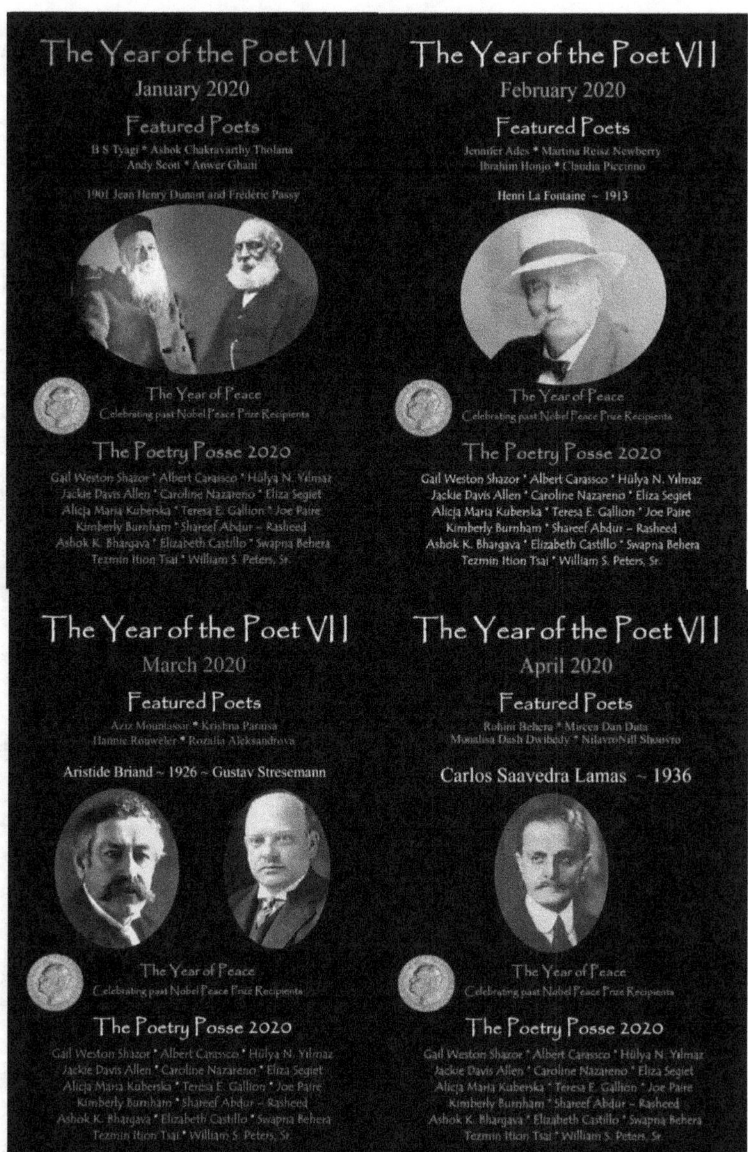
The Year of the Poet VII
January 2020
Featured Poets
B S Tyagi * Ashok Chakravarthy Tholana
Andy Scott * Anwer Ghani
1901 Jean Henry Dunant and Frédéric Passy
The Year of Peace
Celebrating past Nobel Peace Prize Recipients
The Poetry Posse 2020
The Year of the Poet VII
February 2020
Featured Poets
Jennifer Ades * Martina Reisz Newberry
Ibrahim Honjo * Claudia Piccinno
Henri La Fontaine ~ 1913
The Year of Peace
Celebrating past Nobel Peace Prize Recipients
The Poetry Posse 2020
Gail Weston Shazor * Albert Carassco * Hülya N. Yılmaz
Jackie Davis Allen * Caroline Nazareno * Eliza Segiet
Alicja Maria Kuberska * Teresa E. Gallion * Joe Paire
Kimberly Burnham * Shareef Abdur – Rasheed
Ashok K. Bhargava * Elizabeth Castillo * Swapna Behera
Tezmin Ition Tsai * William S. Peters, Sr.
The Year of the Poet VII
March 2020
Featured Poets
Aziz Mountassir * Krishna Parimsa
Hannie Rouweler * Rozalia Aleksandrova
Aristide Briand ~ 1926 ~ Gustav Stresemann
The Year of Peace
Celebrating past Nobel Peace Prize Recipients
The Poetry Posse 2020
The Year of the Poet VII
April 2020
Featured Poets
Rohini Behera * Mircea Dan Duta
Monalisa Dash Dwibedy * NilavroNill Shoovro
Carlos Saavedra Lamas ~ 1936
The Year of Peace
Celebrating past Nobel Peace Prize Recipients
The Poetry Posse 2020

Now Available

www.innerchildpress.com/the-year-of-the-poet

The Year of the Poet VII
May 2020
Featured Poets
Alok Kumar Ray * Eden S. Trinidad
Franco Barbato * Izabela Zubko
Ralph Bunche ~ 1950
The Year of Peace
Celebrating past Nobel Peace Prize Recipients
The Poetry Posse 2020
Gail Weston Shazor * Albert Carassco * Hülya N. Yilmaz
Jackie Davis Allen * Caroline Nazareno * Eliza Segiet
Alicja Maria Kuberska * Teresa E. Gallion * Joe Paire
Kimberly Burnham * Shareef Abdur - Rasheed
Ashok K. Bhargava * Elizabeth Castillo * Swapna Behera
Tezmin Ition Tsai * William S. Peters, Sr.
The Year of the Poet VII
June 2020
Featured Poets
Eftichia Kapardeli * Metin Cengiz
Hussein Habasch * Kosh K Mathew
Albert John Lutuli ~ 1960
The Year of Peace
Celebrating past Nobel Peace Prize Recipients
The Poetry Posse 2020
Gail Weston Shazor * Albert Carassco * Hülya N. Yilmaz
Jackie Davis Allen * Caroline Nazareno * Eliza Segiet
Alicja Maria Kuberska * Teresa E. Gallion * Joe Paire
Kimberly Burnham * Shareef Abdur - Rasheed
Ashok K. Bhargava * Elizabeth Castillo * Swapna Behera
Tezmin Ition Tsai * William S. Peters, Sr.
The Year of the Poet VII
July 2020
Featured Poets
Mykola Martyniuk * Orbindu Ganga
Roula Pollard * Karn Praktisha
Norman Ernest Borlaug ~ 1970
The Year of Peace
Celebrating past Nobel Peace Prize Recipients
The Poetry Posse 2020
Gail Weston Shazor * Albert Carassco * Hülya N. Yilmaz
Jackie Davis Allen * Caroline Nazareno * Eliza Segiet
Alicja Maria Kuberska * Teresa E. Gallion * Joe Paire
Kimberly Burnham * Shareef Abdur - Rasheed
Ashok K. Bhargava * Elizabeth Castillo * Swapna Behera
Tezmin Ition Tsai * William S. Peters, Sr.
The Year of the Poet VII
August 2020
Featured Poets
Dr Pragya Suman * Chinh Nguyen
Srinivas Vasudev * Ugwu Leonard Ifeanyi, Jr.
Adolfo Pérez Esquivel ~ 1980
The Year of Peace
Celebrating past Nobel Peace Prize Recipients
The Poetry Posse 2020
Gail Weston Shazor * Albert Carassco * Hülya N. Yilmaz
Jackie Davis Allen * Caroline Nazareno * Eliza Segiet
Alicja Maria Kuberska * Teresa E. Gallion * Joe Paire
Kimberly Burnham * Shareef Abdur - Rasheed
Ashok K. Bhargava * Elizabeth Castillo * Swapna Behera
Tezmin Ition Tsai * William S. Peters, Sr.

The Year of the Poet VII
September 2020
Featured Poets
Mikhail Sergeyevich Gorbachev ~ 1990
The Year of Peace
Celebrating past Nobel Peace Prize Recipients
The Poetry Posse 2020
The Year of the Poet VII
October 2020
Featured Poets
Mutawaf A. Shaheed * Galina Italyanskaya
Nadeem Fraz * Avril Tanya Meallem
Kim Dae-jung ~ 2000
The Year of Peace
Celebrating past Nobel Peace Prize Recipients
The Poetry Posse 2020
The Year of the Poet VII
November 2020
Featured Poets
Liu Xiaobo ~ 2010
The Year of Peace
Celebrating past Nobel Peace Prize Recipients
The Poetry Posse 2020
The Year of the Poet VII
December 2020
Featured Poets
Ratan Ghosh * Ibtisam Ibrahim Al-Asady
Brindha Vinodh * Selma Kopic
Abiy Ahmed Ali ~ 2019
The Year of Peace
Celebrating past Nobel Peace Prize Recipients
The Poetry Posse 2020
Gail Weston Shazor * Albert Carassco * Hülya N. Yılmaz
Jackie Davis Allen * Caroline Nazareno * Eliza Segiet
Alicja Maria Kuberska * Teresa E. Gallion * Joe Paire
Kimberly Burnham * Shareef Abdur – Rasheed
Ashok K. Bhargava * Elizabeth Castillo * Swapna Behera
Tezmin Ition Tsai * William S. Peters, Sr.

Now Available

www.innerchildpress.com/the-year-of-the-poet

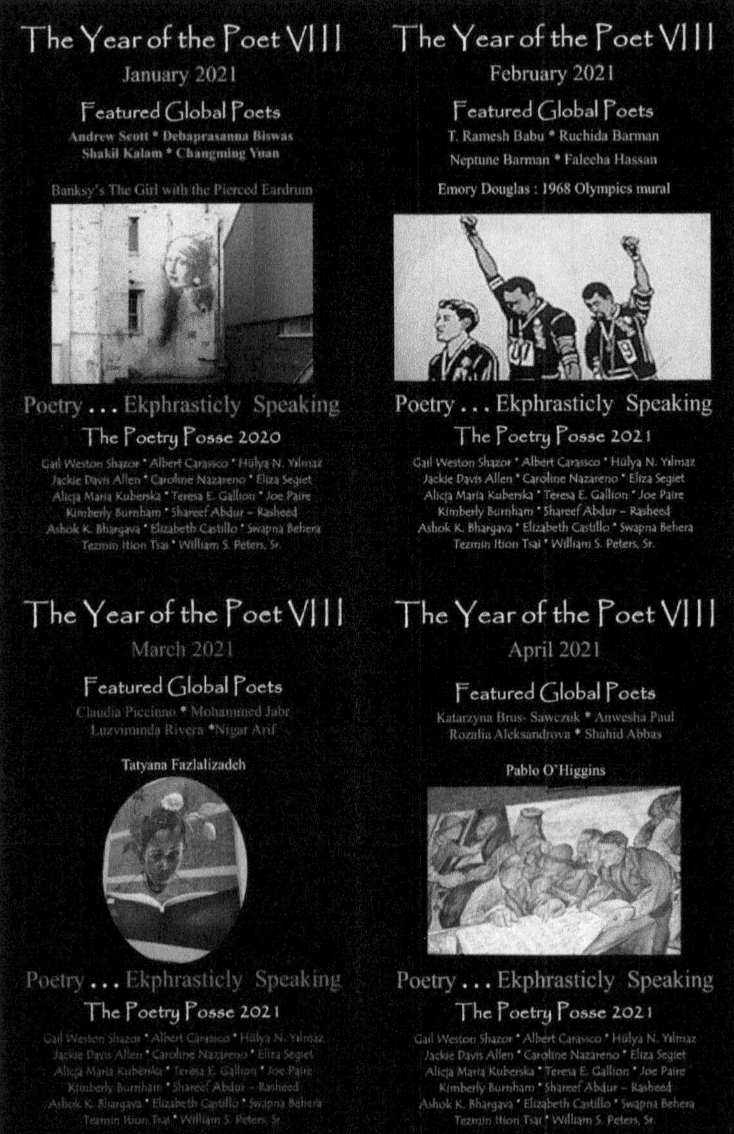
The Year of the Poet VIII
January 2021
Featured Global Poets
Andrew Scott * Debaprasanna Biswas
Shakil Kalam * Changming Yuan
Banksy's The Girl with the Pierced Eardrum
Poetry . . . Ekphrasticly Speaking
The Poetry Posse 2020
Gail Weston Shazor * Albert Carassco * Hülya N. Yılmaz
Jackie Davis Allen * Caroline Nazareno * Eliza Segiet
Alicja Maria Kuberska * Teresa E. Gallion * Joe Paire
Kimberly Burnham * Shareef Abdur – Rasheed
Ashok K. Bhargava * Elizabeth Castillo * Swapna Behera
Tezmin Ition Tsai * William S. Peters, Sr.
The Year of the Poet VIII
February 2021
Featured Global Poets
T. Ramesh Babu * Ruchida Barman
Neptune Barman * Faleeha Hassan
Emory Douglas : 1968 Olympics mural
Poetry . . . Ekphrasticly Speaking
The Poetry Posse 2021
Gail Weston Shazor * Albert Carassco * Hülya N. Yılmaz
Jackie Davis Allen * Caroline Nazareno * Eliza Segiet
Alicja Maria Kuberska * Teresa E. Gallion * Joe Paire
Kimberly Burnham * Shareef Abdur – Rasheed
Ashok K. Bhargava * Elizabeth Castillo * Swapna Behera
Tezmin Ition Tsai * William S. Peters, Sr.
The Year of the Poet VIII
March 2021
Featured Global Poets
Claudia Piccinno * Mohammed Jabr
Luzviminda Rivera *Nigar Arif
Tatyana Fazlalizadeh
Poetry . . . Ekphrasticly Speaking
The Poetry Posse 2021
Gail Weston Shazor * Albert Carassco * Hülya N. Yılmaz
Jackie Davis Allen * Caroline Nazareno * Eliza Segiet
Alicja Maria Kuberska * Teresa E. Gallion * Joe Paire
Kimberly Burnham * Shareef Abdur – Rasheed
Ashok K. Bhargava * Elizabeth Castillo * Swapna Behera
Tezmin Ition Tsai * William S. Peters, Sr.
The Year of the Poet VIII
April 2021
Featured Global Poets
Katarzyna Brus- Sawczuk * Anwesha Paul
Rozalia Aleksandrova * Shahid Abbas
Pablo O'Higgins
Poetry . . . Ekphrasticly Speaking
The Poetry Posse 2021
Gail Weston Shazor * Albert Carassco * Hülya N. Yılmaz
Jackie Davis Allen * Caroline Nazareno * Eliza Segiet
Alicja Maria Kuberska * Teresa E. Gallion * Joe Paire
Kimberly Burnham * Shareef Abdur – Rasheed
Ashok K. Bhargava * Elizabeth Castillo * Swapna Behera
Tezmin Ition Tsai * William S. Peters, Sr.

The Year of the Poet VIII
September 2021
Featured Global Poets
Monsif Beroual * Sandesh Ghimire
Sharmila Poudel * Pavol Janik
Heather Jansch
Poetry . . . Ekphrasticly Speaking
The Poetry Posse 2021
Gail Weston Shazor * Albert Carassco * Hülya N. Yilmaz
Jackie Davis Allen * Caroline Nazareno * Eliza Segiet
Alicja Maria Kuberska * Teresa E. Gallion * Joe Paire
Kimberly Burnham * Shareef Abdur – Rasheed
Ashok K. Bhargava * Elizabeth Castillo * Swapna Behera
Tezmin Ition Tsai * William S. Peters, Sr.
The Year of the Poet VIII
October 2021
Featured Global Poets
C. E. Shy * Saswata Ganguly
Suranjit Gain * Hasiba Hilal
Dale Lamphere
Poetry . . . Ekphrasticly Speaking
The Poetry Posse 2021
Gail Weston Shazor * Albert Carassco * Hülya N. Yilmaz
Jackie Davis Allen * Caroline Nazareno * Eliza Segiet
Alicja Maria Kuberska * Teresa E. Gallion * Joe Paire
Kimberly Burnham * Shareef Abdur – Rasheed
Ashok K. Bhargava * Elizabeth Castillo * Swapna Behera
Tezmin Ition Tsai * William S. Peters, Sr.
The Year of the Poet VIII
November 2021
Featured Global Poets
Errol D. Bean * Ibrahim Honjo
Tanja Ajtic * Rajashree Mohapatra
Andy Goldsworthy
Poetry . . . Ekphrasticly Speaking
The Poetry Posse 2021
Gail Weston Shazor * Albert Carassco * Hülya N. Yilmaz
Jackie Davis Allen * Caroline Nazareno * Eliza Segiet
Alicja Maria Kuberska * Teresa E. Gallion * Joe Paire
Kimberly Burnham * Shareef Abdur – Rasheed
Ashok K. Bhargava * Elizabeth Castillo * Swapna Behera
Tezmin Ition Tsai * William S. Peters, Sr.
The Year of the Poet VIII
December 2021
Featured Global Poets
Orbinda Ganga * Fadairo Tesleem
Anthony Arnold * Iyad Shamasnah
Fredric Edwin Church
Poetry . . . Ekphrasticly Speaking
The Poetry Posse 2021
Gail Weston Shazor * Albert Carassco * Hülya N. Yilmaz
Jackie Davis Allen * Caroline Nazareno * Eliza Segiet
Alicja Maria Kuberska * Teresa E. Gallion * Joe Paire
Kimberly Burnham * Shareef Abdur – Rasheed
Ashok K. Bhargava * Elizabeth Castillo * Swapna Behera
Tezmin Ition Tsai * William S. Peters, Sr.

Now Available

www.innerchildpress.com/the-year-of-the-poet

The Year of the Poet IX
September 2022

Featured Global Poets

Ngozi Olivia Osuoha * Biswajit Mishra
Sylwia K. Malinowska * Sajid Hussein

Climate Change and Wind and Weather Patterns

Poetry ... Ekphrasticly Speaking

The Poetry Posse 2022

Gail Weston Shazor * Albert Carasco * Hülya N. Yılmaz
Jackie Davis Allen * Caroline Nazareno * Eliza Segiet
Alicja Maria Kubenska * Teresa E. Gallion * Joe Paire
Kimberly Burnham * Shareef Abdur – Rasheed
Ashok K. Bhargava * Elizabeth Castillo * Swapna Behera
Tezmin Ition Tsai * William S. Peters, Sr.

The Year of the Poet IX
October 2022

Featured Global Poets

Andrew Kouroupos * Brenda Mohammed
Carthornia Kouroupos * Faleeha Hassan

Climate Change and Oil and Power

Poetry ... Ekphrasticly Speaking

The Poetry Posse 2022

Gail Weston Shazor * Albert Carasco * Hülya N. Yılmaz
Jackie Davis Allen * Caroline Nazareno * Eliza Segiet
Alicja Maria Kubenska * Teresa E. Gallion * Joe Paire
Kimberly Burnham * Shareef Abdur – Rasheed
Ashok K. Bhargava * Elizabeth Castillo * Swapna Behera
Tezmin Ition Tsai * William S. Peters, Sr.

The Year of the Poet IX
November 2022

Featured Global Poets

Hema Ravi * Shafkat Aziz Hajam
Selma Kopic * Ibrahim Honjo

Climate Change : Time to Act

Poetry ... Ekphrasticly Speaking

The Poetry Posse 2022

Gail Weston Shazor * Albert Carasco * Hülya N. Yılmaz
Jackie Davis Allen * Caroline Nazareno * Eliza Segiet
Alicja Maria Kubenska * Teresa E. Gallion * Joe Paire
Kimberly Burnham * Shareef Abdur – Rasheed
Ashok K. Bhargava * Elizabeth Castillo * Swapna Behera
Tezmin Ition Tsai * William S. Peters, Sr.

The Year of the Poet IX
December 2022

Featured Global Poets

Elarbi Abdelfattah * Lorraine Cragg
Neha Bhandarkar * Robert Gibbons

Climate Change Bees, Butterflies and Insect Life

Poetry ... Ekphrasticly Speaking

The Poetry Posse 2022

Gail Weston Shazor * Albert Carasco * Hülya N. Yılmaz
Jackie Davis Allen * Caroline Nazareno * Eliza Segiet
Alicja Maria Kubenska * Teresa E. Gallion * Joe Paire
Kimberly Burnham * Shareef Abdur – Rasheed
Ashok K. Bhargava * Elizabeth Castillo * Swapna Behera
Tezmin Ition Tsai * William S. Peters, Sr.

Now Available

www.innerchildpress.com/the-year-of-the-poet

The Year of the Poet X
January 2023
Featured Global Poets
JuNe Barefield * Swayam Prashant
Willow Rose * Shabbirhusein K Jamnagerwalla
Children : Difference Makers

Iqbal Masih

The Poetry Posse 2023
Gail Weston Shazor * Albert Carassco * Hülya N. Yılmaz
Jackie Davis Allen * Caroline Nazareno * Kimberly Burnham
Alicja Maria Kuberska * Teresa E. Gallion * Joe Paire
Michelle Joan Barulich * Shareef Abdur – Rasheed
Ashok K. Bhargava * Elizabeth Castillo * Swapna Behera
Tezmin Ition Tsai * Eliza Segiet * William S. Peters, Sr.

The Year of the Poet X
February 2023
Featured Global Poets
Christena Williams * Hilda Graciela Kraft
Francesco Favetta * Dr. H.C. Louise Hudon
Children : Difference Makers

Ruby Bridges

The Poetry Posse 2023
Gail Weston Shazor * Albert Carassco * Hülya N. Yılmaz
Jackie Davis Allen * Caroline Nazareno * Kimberly Burnham
Alicja Maria Kuberska * Teresa E. Gallion * Joe Paire
Michelle Joan Barulich * Shareef Abdur – Rasheed
Ashok K. Bhargava * Elizabeth Castillo * Swapna Behera
Tezmin Ition Tsai * Eliza Segiet * William S. Peters, Sr.

The Year of the Poet X
March 2023
Featured Global Poets
Clarena Martinez Turizo * Binod Dawadi
Til Kumari Sharma * Petrouchka Alexieva
Children : Difference Makers

Yo Yo Ma

The Poetry Posse 2023
Gail Weston Shazor * Albert Carassco * Hülya N. Yılmaz
Jackie Davis Allen * Caroline Nazareno * Kimberly Burnham
Alicja Maria Kuberska * Teresa E. Gallion * Joe Paire
Michelle Joan Barulich * Shareef Abdur – Rasheed
Ashok K. Bhargava * Elizabeth Castillo * Swapna Behera
Tezmin Ition Tsai * Eliza Segiet * William S. Peters, Sr.

The Year of the Poet X
April 2023
Featured Global Poets
Maxwanette A Poetess * Alonzo Gross
Türkan Ergör * Ibrahim Honjo
Children : Difference Makers

Claudette Colvin

The Poetry Posse 2023
Gail Weston Shazor * Albert Carassco * Hülya N. Yılmaz
Jackie Davis Allen * Caroline Nazareno * Kimberly Burnham
Alicja Maria Kuberska * Teresa E. Gallion * Joe Paire
Michelle Joan Barulich * Shareef Abdur – Rasheed
Ashok K. Bhargava * Elizabeth Castillo * Swapna Behera
Tezmin Ition Tsai * Eliza Segiet * William S. Peters, Sr.

Now Available

www.innerchildpress.com/the-year-of-the-poet

The Year of the Poet X
May 2023
Csp Shrivastava * Michael Lee Johnson
Taghrid Bou Merhi * Yasmin Brown
Children : Difference Makers
Louis Braille
The Poetry Posse 2023
The Year of the Poet X
June 2023
Featured Global Poets
Kay Peters * Carthornia Kouroupos
Andrew Kouroupos * Faleeha Hassan
Children : Difference Makers
Ryan Hreljac
The Poetry Posse 2023
The Year of the Poet X
July 2023
Featured Global Poets
Rajashree Mohapatra * Biswajit Mishra
Johan Karlsson * Teodozja Świderska
Children : Difference Makers
~ Bana al-Abed ~
The Poetry Posse 2023
Gail Weston Shazor * Albert Carassco * Hülya N. Yılmaz
Jackie Davis Allen * Caroline Nazareno * Kimberly Burnham
Alicja Maria Kuberska * Teresa E. Gallion * Joe Paire
Michelle Joan Barulich * Shareef Abdur – Rasheed
Ashok K. Bhargava * Elizabeth Castillo * Swapna Behera
Tezmin Ition Tsai * Eliza Segiet * William S. Peters, Sr.
The Year of the Poet X
August 2023
Featured Global Poets
Kennedy Wanda Ochieng * Jose Lopez
Sylwia K. Malinowska * Laurent Grison
Children : Difference Makers
~ Kelvin Doe ~
The Poetry Posse 2023
Gail Weston Shazor * Albert Carassco * Hülya N. Yılmaz
Jackie Davis Allen * Caroline Nazareno * Kimberly Burnham
Alicja Maria Kuberska * Teresa E. Gallion * Joe Paire
Michelle Joan Barulich * Shareef Abdur – Rasheed
Ashok K. Bhargava * Elizabeth Castillo * Swapna Behera
Tezmin Ition Tsai * Eliza Segiet * William S. Peters, Sr.

Now Available

www.innerchildpress.com/the-year-of-the-poet

The Year of the Poet X
September 2023
Featured Global Poets
Eftichia Karpadeli * Chinh Nguyen
Nigar Agalarova * Carmela Cueva
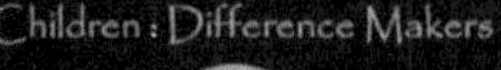
Children : Difference Makers

~ Easton LaChappelle ~
The Poetry Posse 2023
Gail Weston Shazor * Albert Carassco * Hülya N. Yılmaz
Jackie Davis Allen * Caroline Nazareno * Kimberly Burnham
Alicja Maria Kuberska * Teresa E. Gallion * Joe Paire
Michelle Joan Barulich * Shareef Abdur – Rasheed
Ashok K. Bhargava * Elizabeth Castillo * Swapna Behera
Tezmin Ition Tsai * Eliza Segiet * William S. Peters, Sr.

The Year of the Poet X
October 2023
Featured Global Poets
CSP Shrivastava * Huniie Parker
Noreen Snyder * Ramkrishna Paul
Children : Difference Makers

~ Malala Yousafzai ~
The Poetry Posse 2023
Gail Weston Shazor * Albert Carassco * Hülya N. Yılmaz
Jackie Davis Allen * Caroline Nazareno * Kimberly Burnham
Alicja Maria Kuberska * Teresa E. Gallion * Joe Paire
Michelle Joan Barulich * Shareef Abdur – Rasheed
Ashok K. Bhargava * Elizabeth Castillo * Swapna Behera
Tezmin Ition Tsai * Eliza Segiet * William S. Peters, Sr.

The Year of the Poet X
November 2023
Featured Global Poets
Ibrahim Honjo * Balachandran Nair
Xanthi Hondrou-Hil * Francesco Favetta
Children : Difference Makers

~ Jean-Michel Basquiat ~
The Poetry Posse 2023
Gail Weston Shazor * Albert Carassco * Hülya N. Yılmaz
Jackie Davis Allen * Caroline Nazareno * Kimberly Burnham
Alicja Maria Kuberska * Teresa E. Gallion * Joe Paire
Michelle Joan Barulich * Shareef Abdur – Rasheed
Ashok K. Bhargava * Elizabeth Castillo * Swapna Behera
Tezmin Ition Tsai * Eliza Segiet * William S. Peters, Sr.

The Year of the Poet X
December 2023
Featured Global Poets
Caroline Laurent Turunc * Neha Bhandarkar
Shafkat Aziz Hajam * Elarbi Abdelfattah
Children : Difference Makers

~ Melati and Isabel Wijsen ~
The Poetry Posse 2023
Gail Weston Shazor * Albert Carassco * Hülya N. Yılmaz
Jackie Davis Allen * Caroline Nazareno * Kimberly Burnham
Alicja Maria Kuberska * Teresa E. Gallion * Joe Paire
Michelle Joan Barulich * Shareef Abdur – Rasheed
Ashok K. Bhargava * Elizabeth Castillo * Swapna Behera
Tezmin Ition Tsai * Eliza Segiet * William S. Peters, Sr.

Now Available

www.innerchildpress.com/the-year-of-the-poet

The Year of the Poet XI
January 2024
Featured Global Poets
Til Kumari Sharma * Shafkat Aziz Hajam
Daniela Marian * Eleni Vassiliou – Asteroskon
Renowned Poets
~ Phyllis Wheatley ~
The Poetry Posse 2024
Gail Weston Shazor * Albert Carassco * Hülya N. Yılmaz
Jackie Davis Allen * Caroline Nazareno * Mutawaf Shaheed
Alicja Maria Kuberska * Teresa E. Gallion * Noreen Snyder
Michelle Joan Barulich * Shareef Abdur – Rasheed
Ashok K. Bhargava * Elizabeth Castillo * Swapna Behera
Tezmin Ition Tsai * Eliza Segiet * William S. Peters, Sr.
The Year of the Poet XI
February 2024
Featured Global Poets
Caroline Laurent Turunç * Julio Pavanetti
Lidia Chiarelli * Lina Buividavičiūtė
Renowned Poets
~ Omar Khayyam ~
The Poetry Posse 2024
Gail Weston Shazor * Albert Carassco * Hülya N. Yılmaz
Jackie Davis Allen * Caroline Nazareno * Mutawaf Shaheed
Alicja Maria Kuberska * Teresa E. Gallion * Noreen Snyder
Michelle Joan Barulich * Shareef Abdur – Rasheed
Ashok K. Bhargava * Elizabeth Castillo * Swapna Behera
Tezmin Ition Tsai * Eliza Segiet * William S. Peters, Sr.
The Year of the Poet XI
March 2024
Featured Global Poets
Francesco Favetta * Jagjit Singh Zandu
Carmela Núñez Yukimura Peruana * Michael Lee Johnson
Renowned Poets
~ Nâzim Hikmet ~
The Poetry Posse 2024
Gail Weston Shazor * Albert Carassco * Hülya N. Yılmaz
Jackie Davis Allen * Caroline Nazareno * Mutawaf Shaheed
Alicja Maria Kuberska * Teresa E. Gallion * Noreen Snyder
Michelle Joan Barulich * Shareef Abdur – Rasheed
Ashok K. Bhargava * Elizabeth Castillo * Swapna Behera
Tezmin Ition Tsai * Eliza Segiet * William S. Peters, Sr.
The Year of the Poet XI
April 2024
Featured Global Poets
Hassanal Abdullah * Johny Takkedasila
Rajashree Mohapatra * Shirley Smothers
Renowned Poets
~ William Butler Yeats ~
The Poetry Posse 2024
Gail Weston Shazor * Albert Carassco Hülya N. Yılmaz
Jackie Davis Allen * Caroline Nazareno * Mutawaf Shaheed
Alicja Maria Kuberska * Teresa E. Gallion * Noreen Snyder
Michelle Joan Barulich * Shareef Abdur – Rasheed
Ashok K. Bhargava * Elizabeth Castillo * Swapna Behera
Tezmin Ition Tsai * Eliza Segiet * William S. Peters, Sr.

Now Available

www.innerchildpress.com/the-year-of-the-poet

and there is much, much more !

visit . . .

www.innerchildpress.com/anthologies-sales-special.php

Also check out our Authors and all the wonderful Books Available at :

www.innerchildpress.com/authors-pages

INNER CHILD PRESS
WORLD HEALING
WORLD PEACE
2018
A Poetry Anthology for Humanity

i support
World Healing
World Peace

www.worldhealingworldpeacepoetry.com

World Healing World Peace
PoEtRy
i am a believer !

World Healing World Peace

2012, 2014, 2016, 2018, 2020, 2022

Now Available

www.worldhealingworldpeacepoetry.com

Inner Child Press International

'building bridges of cultural understanding'

Meet the Board of Directors

William S. Peters, Sr.
Chair Person
Founder
Inner Child Enterprises
Inner Child Press

Hülya N Yılmaz
Director
Editing Services
Co-Chair Person

Fahredin B. Shehu
Director
Cultural Affairs

Elizabeth E. Castillo
Director
Recording Secretary

De'Andre Hawthorne
Director
Performance Poetry

Gail Weston Shazor
Director
Anthologies

Kimberly Burnham
Director
Cultural Ambassador
Pacific Northwest
USA

Ashok K. Bhargava
Director
WIN Awards

Deborah Smart
Director
Publicity
Marketing

www.innerchildpress.com

Inner Child Press International

'building bridges of cultural understanding'

Meet our Cultural Ambassadors

Fahredin Shehu
Director of Cultural
Kosovo

Faleha Hassan
Iraq – USA

Elizabeth E. Castillo
Philippines

Antoinette Coleman
Chicago
Midwest USA

Ananda Nepali
Nepal – East
Northern India

Kimberly Burnham
Pacific Northwest
USA

Alicja Kuberska
Poland
Eastern Europe

Swapna Behera
India
Southeast Asia

Kolade O. Freedom
Nigeria
West Africa

Monsif Beroual
Morocco
Northern Africa

Ashok K. Bhargava
Canada

Tzemin Ition Tsai
Republic of China
Greater China

Alicia M. Ramírez
Mexico
Central America

Christena AV Williams
Jamaica
Caribbean

Louise Hudon
Eastern Canada

Aziz Mountassir
Morocco
Northern Africa

Shareef Abdur-Rasheed
Southeastern USA

Laure Charazac
France
Western Europe

Mohammad Ikbal Harb
Lebanon
Middle East

Mohamed Abdel Aziz Shmeis
Egypt
Middle East

Hilary Mainga
Kenya
Eastern Africa

Josephus R. Johnson
Liberia

Mennadi Farah
Algeria

Marlon Salem Gruezo
Philippines

www.innerchildpress.com

This Anthological Publication
is underwritten solely by

Inner Child Press International

Inner Child Press is a Publishing Company Founded and Operated by Writers. Our personal publishing experiences provides us an intimate understanding of the sometimes daunting challenges Writers, New and Seasoned may face in the Business of Publishing and Marketing their Creative "Written Work".

For more Information

Inner Child Press International

www.innerchildpress.com

Inner Child Press International
'building bridges of cultural understanding'
202 Wiltree Court, State College, Pennsylvania 16801
www.innerchildpress.com

~ fini ~

www.ingramcontent.com/pod-product-compliance
Lightning Source LLC
LaVergne TN
LVHW051041080426
835508LV00019B/1649

* 9 7 8 1 9 6 1 4 9 8 2 5 9 *